Customer Relationship Management

Customer Relationship Management

How To Develop and Execute a CRM Strategy

Michael Pearce FIC CMC

BEP

BUSINESS EXPERT PRESS

Leader in applied, concise business books

Customer Relationship Management:
How To Develop and Execute a CRM Strategy

Copyright © Business Expert Press, LLC, 2021.

Cover design by Charlene Kronstedt

Interior design by Exeter Premedia Services Private Ltd., Chennai, India

First published in 2021 by
Business Expert Press, LLC
222 East 46th Street, New York, NY 10017
www.businessexpertpress.com

ISBN-13: 978-1-95334-964-4 (paperback)
ISBN-13: 978-1-95334-965-1 (e-book)

Business Expert Press Marketing Collection

Collection ISSN: 2169-3978 (print)
Collection ISSN: 2169-3986 (electronic)

First edition: 2021

10 9 8 7 6 5 4 3 2 1

Description

CRM first entered the business vocabulary in the early 90's; initially as a systems driven technical solution. It has since escalated in importance as system providers increased their market penetration of the business market and, in parallel, CRM's strategic importance gained more traction as it was recognized that CRM was, at its heart, a business model in the pursuit of sustainable profit.

This was accentuated by the academic community stepping up their interest in the subject in the early 2000's. Today, it is a universal business topic which has been re-engineered by the online shopping revolution in which the customer is firmly placed at the center of the business. The current reality, however, is that, for the vast majority of businesses, CRM has not been adopted as a business philosophy and practicing business model. It has not been fully understood and therefore fully embraced and properly implemented.

The author addresses this head-on by stripping CRM down into its component parts by delving into and explaining the role and relevance of the C, R, and M in CRM. This is a practical guide but set within a strategic framework. The outage is clear actionable insights and how to convert them into delivery. It is written in an easily digestible, non-jargon style, with case studies to demonstrate how CRM works. This book can be immediately used as the primary practical reference to guide the development and implementation of a CRM strategy.

Keywords

customer relationship management; CRM; relationship marketing; customer loyalty; targeted marketing; customer centric business model; database management; data mining; brand proposition; brand positioning; customer centric database; cloud based CRM systems; customer profitability; customer segmentation; ROI; CRM strategy

Contents

Acknowledgments

To everyone I have met in my consultancy and business career who have helped shape my thinking on CRM as a business model fit for modern times, in which the customer should be at the center of all companies' strategic planning. In particular, my thanks to friends and colleagues in Adactus who created the "space" and provided support to enable me to write this book.

CHAPTER 1

Introduction

Like many management innovations, a multitude of spins on the subject often rapidly emerge and can create distortions, myths, and misunderstanding of the true application and worth of the innovation.

CRM is no exception. Firstly, it is neither new nor an innovation. Any marketing orientated company can vouch for that where the customer has always been the center of their universe, and continuously seeking out and meeting customer needs (if not their wants) their mantra.

Secondly, the thrust of the drive to put CRM on the management agenda has largely been through software companies' marketing proprietary CRM systems. Certainly these systems have made a real step change in data processing in capturing, storing, marshalling, analyzing, and applying data to enhance decision making. More importantly, they handle "big data" and supply it in a highly relevant way to all user groups who have customer touch points, to help enrich the customer experience. *But, they are not CRM itself.* They are one of the tools in the CRM toolbox. For sure they are a really important one and a key component of the CRM strategic operational framework, but CRM systems are processes. They are an integral part of the CRM strategy but not the strategy itself.

So, let's start by stripping down CRM to give an overview and identify and understand its role in a business.

Customer Relationship Management (CRM) relates to acquiring, developing, and retaining satisfied loyal customers. To achieve sustainable profitable growth, it is generally desirable for a company to increase the number of profitable customers, to increase the profit from existing customers, and to extend the duration of the customers' relationship with the company (or brand).

In today's increasingly competitive business environment, a fundamental change has taken place. The emerging global and electronic economy has turned tradition on its head and, for consumer markets, placed the customer firmly in the driving seat: as a result of which, power has irreversibly shifted from the seller to the customer with customer choice (and competition) one Google search away. Customers are more demanding, more aware of their choices, and more in command than ever before. Add the fact that cost cutting alone will not generate long-term profit growth, it is clear that CRM is an enterprise wide imperative.

However, many companies are not ideally positioned to capitalize on the opportunity for customer-oriented growth. While some companies have made attempts to implement CRM solutions (frequently by installing CRM systems rather than adopting a top-down CRM strategy), they have often not transformed themselves into customer-driven enterprises. The actual results can be more a set of disconnected initiatives that fall short of creating real value.

A holistic approach is required for CRM to allow a company to orchestrate all the activities that bring it into contact with its customers to deliver a consistently differentiated—and personalized—customer experience regardless of the interactive channel chosen by the customer, embracing their experience with all touch points with the company. Such an approach can permit companies to knit together marketing, sales, and service functions that would have traditionally been pursued (are pursued) in separate ad hoc ways, and therefore, constitutes a more comprehensive, methodical approach to identifying, attracting, and retaining the most valuable customers.

CRM is therefore best described as a business philosophy; as a modern day approach to manage profitability by placing the customer at the center of the business. By definition, it is a corporate strategic approach and, as such, is driven by the Board of Directors with its impact company wide as to how it organizes itself to fully practice CRM.

About This Book

Welcome to the first edition of "CRM: How to Develop and Execute a CRM Strategy". This book explains all the facets of CRM; its definition, its strategic role and application, and the approach to developing a successful CRM strategy through breaking it down into its constituent parts from both conceptual and practical perspectives.

It is intended to provide a guide to developing and implementing a successful CRM strategy in its primary commercial role of optimizing profit over the long term.

CRM is customer centric. As such it is relevant to both B2C and B2B business models with its application reflecting the customer profile and segmentation of the operating company within its market sector.

However, the references and case studies in the book are slanted toward B2C but this should not detract from all parties subscribing to the principles and practices embodied in the CRM approach to business management.

In this context, it should also be noted that the B2C model has a number of variants; of which, the primary ones are:

- Many B2C producers/suppliers of manufactured goods and service providers (e.g., insurance products) reach their ultimate customer (the consumer of their product or service) through intermediaries—wholesalers, retailers, and agents—who are their primary customers to whom they sell and invoice. This adds an extra layer of complexity with two strands of "customers." CRM applies to both audiences with policies entwined between the two with an integrated approach.
- Of course, the buying customer and consumer can be one and the same. This is the relationship enjoyed by retailers and their "shoppers" as well as those selling products and services online directly to the consumer.

In conclusion, CRM relates to all business models and I encourage all senior company managers to fully interrogate its application to their individual circumstances and, thereafter, completely embrace it. I sincerely hope this book stimulates you to embark on the CRM journey, if you have not already done so, and helps guide you on the way to a successful end. For those who have started the journey, I hope it acts as a refresher and reminder of all the facets of CRM and acts as a check list as to whether you have been faithful to the CRM charter and helps you make the right corrections if you have deviated from it.

Finally and importantly, the book puts a pragmatic perspective on CRM because CRM is not an erudite, theoretical model. It is how business should operate in the modern trading world in the pursuit of sustainable long-term profits to maximize shareholder value.

As such, the thrust of the book is to provide practical and actionable guidelines to developing and executing a CRM strategy. It is supported by case studies selected to highlight key aspects of CRM with a common theme of focusing on the commercial benefits to be gained from implementing a successful CRM approach to business. They use quantitative empirical evidence related to the dynamics and metrics that drive a business. They are based on companies operating in the United Kingdom (UK) market sectors but, to a large extent, the reader can put this to one side and focus on what the case studies are saying. The insights and conclusions illustrated in each one can be applied to any set of free market conditions.

Summary

In summary, the book moves through the gears from the principles applying to CRM to the operational in the following steps:

Chapter 2 logically starts with the definition of CRM by interrogating and dissecting all the various definitions expunged across academia and the business world to arrive at a clear workable definition.

Chapter 3 addresses the history and evolution of CRM being originally born out of the definition of marketing. In doing so, it highlights two strands of thought that have contributed to the CRM crusade: market changes underpinning CRM and the process of Relationship Marketing.

Chapter 4 lays down the tramlines for developing a CRM strategy. A major disciplined exercise that needs to be undertaken with the clear and unequivocal mission to develop a strategic CRM business model based on **FACTS,** using quantified analysis as the foundation for sound decision making.

To reflect this, it comprehensively sets out the customer analysis required to identify the sources of revenue and profit across the customer base in building a customer segmentation model, which in turn underpins the strategy itself. Thereafter, it identifies the factors crucial to the successful implementation of the CRM strategy embracing technology, processes, and people.

The chapter ends with two case studies to demonstrate CRM strategies as working models.

Chapter 5 is customer centric. CRM starts and ends with the customer. The **CUSTOMER IS KING** and the number 1 marketing commandment is "KNOW YOUR CUSTOMER." This chapter thoroughly and incisively dissects the customer challenge at the center of CRM under the following headings:

A. "The customer rules the roost: the case for placing the customer at the epicenter of the business."

B. What information to gather and how to collect it?

- Who are they?
- What is their buying behavior?
- What are the reasons behind their buying behavior?
- Identifying and fully understanding their needs and wants, and the degree to which your brand meets these relative to competition.

C. The key output can be classified as the "The Holy Grail"— defining the Brand Proposition. Given its external importance, a "Brand Positioning Statement" is featured based on a brand in the restaurant sector. This provides a practical guide for readers to potentially use as the blueprint for building their own if they do not have one in place.

Chapter 6 places the definition of brand loyalty under the microscope and the related importance of building an emotional bond between the brand and its customers through an emotional bridge. This is the territory of Relationship Marketing and is the "R" in CRM.

Maximizing profit through developing ongoing loyalty among "best prospect customers" sits at the heart of CRM. But what is loyalty and how do we nurture and own it? This chapter explores this priority subject area under the following headings:

- Why is loyalty important?
- What is loyalty?
- Who to build a relationship with?

- How to build a relationship—Relationship Marketing?
- What steps should be taken?
- What loyalty programs will be offered?

Chapter 7 addresses the technical aspects of CRM whilst acknowledging that "CRM is a business strategy—not a technology." For CRM to succeed in a company, first develop your CRM strategy and then choose the best technology to support it.

The technical CRM system solution is essential to the successful implementation of a CRM strategy. It is effectively the "engine room" of the data flow network and is an integral part of process management, which, if properly organized, significantly contributes to enhancing the customer experience at all touch points with the brand.

This is, in essence, the "M" in CRM and, given its high ranking status, is comprehensively covered in the chapter under the following headings:

- The Macro Picture
- CRM system features
- CRM system benefits
- CRM system solution specification
- Role of Customer Centric Database
- Types of CRM systems
- Benefits of Cloud based system
- Service Level Agreement (SLA)
- Some practicalities
- Advice and guidance from a "technical expert"

Chapter 8 covers B2B. All the CRM principles and practices apply to both B2C and B2B models but B2B even more so. In B2B, the company is dealing directly with the primary customer who purchases the product or service and, given this, a complete sales history is available for each customer.

This chapter acknowledges this and identifies and breaks down the customer facing processes to define their roles and contribution to customer management. This includes defining the target audience (and isolating the complexities of decision making in many customers), lead management, customer support, sales pipeline management, and scoping the sales operation.

Chapter 9 summarizes the key principles and practical steps that should be fully taken on board to successfully develop and implement a CRM strategy. It consolidates the learnings from the previous chapters.

Chapter 10 summarizes the commercial and working practice benefits that a successful CRM strategy can deliver—THE ULTIMATE PRIZE.

Chapter 11 provides some useful measurement definitions and formulae on metrics relevant to CRM business practices.

CHAPTER 2

Definition*1

There have been a number of definitions quoted from the 1990s when CRM first came onto the radar screen, and since then, it has entered the regular vocabulary of business. It is worth visiting and exploring these prior to focusing on the definition I will be using as the focal point for this book.

Let us start by tabling some of the CRM "sound bites" of comments commonly aired within the business and academic worlds:

1. Information technology companies have tended to use the term CRM to describe the software applications that are used to support the marketing, selling, and service functions of business. It's a technology used to manage interactions with customers and potential customers at each stage of the customer journey from initial recruitment through to optimizing customer development; manifesting itself in the retention of key customer segments who contribute most value to the company P & L.

   The technical CRM system is a tool that is used for contact management, sales management, and customer service. It captures, stores, marshals and organizes data to provide users with quantified, accurate customer information to enhance decision making, whilst enriching the customer experience with all touch points with the company by making them more personal with up-to-date individual records.

   All the customer data is held in one place to give a single customer view (SCV) and outputting data into a simple, customizable dashboard that can tell company personnel a customer's personal profile, their previous contact and purchasing history with the company, their buying preferences, the status of their orders, any outstanding customer service issues, and so on.

2. CRM is the process of customer management. A CRM system digitizes processes and automates tasks to improve the efficiency and efficacy of customer relationship management. CRM streamlines processes and makes customer information available to all the personnel who have contact with the customer in a readily accessible form. It implements customer centric processes to nurture and manage customer relationships covering all the aspects of interaction a company has with its customers, including prospecting, sales, service, and their contact status in line with the data protection regulations in the operating region(s). In the UK, these are the "General Data Protection Regulation (GDPR)."

3. Customer Relationship Management is a phrase that describes how a business interacts with its customers. Most people think of CRM as a system to capture and process information about its customers in a highly efficient and effective manner. However, that is only part of the story. Using technology to gather the intelligence a company needs to provide improved support and services to its customers is "base camp." The critical factor is how the information captured is used to better understand a company's customers and their needs and applying that insight to identify new customers and maximize the life time value of existing customers resulting in higher profits. Analysis, interpretation, and insights derived from the customer data are fundamental to maximizing the potential commercial benefits in successfully implementing a CRM strategy.

   When implemented successfully, CRM gives companies not only insight into the opportunities to grow business with each customer, but also a way of measuring their value.

4. Although some people think of CRM as just a technology, it is so much more than that. No technology, no matter how sophisticated, can be successful without a strategy to direct its implementation and application. Business strategy and technology must work together to bring a customer centric plan to life.

   CRM is a business philosophy about how relationships with customers and potential customers should be managed in the pursuit of profit. Simply expressed, it is putting the customers first and building an enterprise around them.

CRM is a strategic approach to business that is concerned with creating improved shareholder value through the development of appropriate relationships with key customers and customer segments. CRM unites the potential of relationship marketing strategies and IT to create profitable, long-term relationships with customers and other key stakeholders. CRM provides enhanced opportunities to use data and information to both understand customers and co-create value with them. This requires a cross functional integration of processes, people, operations, and marketing capabilities that is enabled through information technology and applications.

It is a companywide business strategy designed to improve revenues and profitability, improve efficiencies and reduce related costs, and optimize customer loyalty, particularly among the most valuable and profitable customers.

In summary, there are three important interlocked strands to CRM in practice: CRM systems and CRM analytical tools supporting the CRM strategy.

CRM Systems

In simple terms, CRM systems integrate and harness data to efficiently and effectively manage customer relationships.

CRM systems are expensive to install, support, and apply. In this context, based on practical observation and experience, I table a set of guidelines to follow both before you decide to commit to a CRM system and running the system post installation:

1. A statement of the obvious perhaps, but fundamentally decide on the system's role(s) in the business up front and, in doing so, lay down the functional specification that the system is required to meet. This is not a "back of a fag packet" exercise and, whatever you do, do not let the seller of the system dictate what you need.

   This is a serious project involving all stakeholders in the business. A project leader should be appointed with the key output being a written functional specification. This should be signed off by all user groups (sales, marketing, customer service, IT, finance) before being confirmed by the Board.

The functional specification should then be used as the sole reference point in discussion with potential suppliers of proprietary and bespoke systems. It is likely that proprietary systems will contain functional features that you simply do not need and, as such, you should take this into account in making your combined cost and benefit assessments of the alternative system solutions. This stage will yield the capital and operational costs, together with the installation plan. It is important that any additional costs are identified and allowed for as a direct consequence of installing the system. For example, running parallel systems until the new system is tested and validated and signed off as being "fit for purpose."

A final financial written operational assessment should be made with a full cost and benefit evaluation and payback, which is formally presented and signed off by the Board.

I cannot emphasize enough the need for a rigorous and robust approach with three major commercial benefits:

A. Make sure you get what you need and not for things that come under the "nice to have" banner.

B. Remember you are the customer. It is vital to have a written specification to measure the supplier's performance and delivery against, which, in so doing, gives you the upper hand if and when the supplier comes back to negotiate a higher fee!

C. It provides the main project management tool for the appointed Project Manager to deliver the project on time to budget.

2. A good system will capture and marshal customer data and make it available in an easily digestible and accessible form. Customer data is "richer" on dimensions of breadth and depth. However, the true commercial prize is how you apply the data. This means, the relevant personnel resource needs to be expanded alongside the installation of the system. To positively use the data to enhance decision making by, for example, developing customer segmentation programs in communicating targeted messaging at the right

time to the right customers, thereby making communication more relevant and personal resulting in a higher level of engagement and response. This can only be realized if the appropriate resource is in place to extract the maximum commercial gain.

From observation, this does not universally happen with, for example, companies not expanding the marketing resource, which effectively nullifies the potential financial benefit and, in turn, fails to deliver a return on the cost of putting in the system.

I believe the level of human resource required to make the optimal commercial use of the CRM system should be identified and the associated cost incorporated as part of the financial justification for installing a CRM system. If not, you will definitively not derive the potential commercial benefit available from such a system.

CRM Analytical Tools

Succinctly put, CRM analytical tools collate and analyze customer data collected through multiple sources and present it so that business managers can make more informed, more quantified decisions.

Companies, particularly large companies, can gather and store a large amount of customer data but the trick is how to convert raw data into useful, actionable knowledge. To extract insights from the data gathered and translate these into enhanced decision making.

There are a number of techniques available from the simple (e.g., multi-variable analysis, correlation) to the more complex. The "bigger the data," the more the need to apply **Data Mining**—the process that uses statistical, mathematical, artificial intelligence, and machine learning techniques to extract, identify, and analyze useful information to subsequently gain knowledge from large databases.

Data Mining is a relevant tool for analyzing customer data to identify valuable information, make better decisions, and generate targeted opportunities based on customer characteristics. Data Mining is based on selecting the primary data sets and breaking them down through the use of techniques such as classification, pattern recognition, and clustering.

CRM Strategy

CRM is a business strategy, not a technology. For CRM to succeed in your company, first develop your CRM strategy and then choose the best technology to support it.

In summary, CRM is a business philosophy—a company wide business strategy organized with the customer at its center with the singular commercial objective of optimizing revenues and profit through focusing on customer development and increasing their loyalty.

As such, it starts and ends with the Board of Directors. It is "top-down" and embraces and impacts the company structure, its organization, its systems and processes, and, most of all, its culture and ethos.

Given that it is a customer centric business strategy, there are some key foundations to have in place to underpin it:

1. To segment the customer base to identify the sources of revenue and profit as the basis for resource allocation and priority setting. The "pareto" principle applies to most businesses, if not all, that 20 percent of customers account for 80 percent of revenue. In reality, it may be more like 30/70 but the principle remains a valid one— **"All customers are equal but some are more equal than others."**

2. To report profit by customer segment. In simple terms, profit = revenue – costs. Customer demand is the determinant of revenue and, as such, it is important to understand which customer segments are contributing most to revenue and whether the appropriate level of company resources are allocated to their development. This should be reported at Board Level alongside the normal operating profit statements. More importantly, KPIs (Key Performance Indicators) should be set by customer segment.

3. Implement the most appropriate technology in support of the strategy, including defining the customer data to be collected and stored. In addition, identify how you are going to use the benefits offered by the technology wisely to help build customer relationships and customer experience. For example, for a hotel to provide profiles of all customers due to arrive and check in that day to the front-of house reception staff to afford a more personalized welcome.

Reference Definition

"CRM is a customer centric business strategy that seeks to optimize customer development, revenues and profit.

It segments the customer base to identify the sources of revenue and profit contribution as the basis for resource allocation, objective setting and strategic planning.

It uses technology and processes to integrate and marshal customer data as the primary data source, supplemented by external data, and to manage all relationships and interactions with customers and potential customers with the aim of enhancing customer experiences."

I use this as my guiding reference in the following chapters.

*(act.com, What is CRM? accessed March 5, 2020), (Baran, Zerres and Zerres, Customer Relationship Management, Bookboon.com, accessed May 30, 2019), (DHL Masterclass.com, accessed December 15, 2019), (Innovation PEI – Province of Ontario, Customer Relationship Management, 2013, accessed May 15, 2019), (Jennifer Lund, What is CRM? The Definitive Guide to Success, Superoffice.com, accessed April 23, 2019), (Rouse, Ehrens, and Kiwak, CRM – customer relationship management, WhatIs.com, accessed April 23, 2019), (Salesforce.com, What is CRM?, accessed April 23, 2019), (Wikipedia, s.v.v. "Customer – relationship management", accessed April 23, 2019, https://en.wikipedia.org/wiki/customer-relationship_management)

Some Key Thoughts to Reflect on if You Are Considering/Reviewing CRM

Where are you on the CRM journey? If at the beginning, internally debate and agree the CRM definition you will use as your ongoing reference, which can also be translated into your CRM vision. If you have already embarked on the CRM path, are you working as a collective to a CRM definition and vision? If so, how does it match up to the strategic definition cited above, or is it more slanted toward processes and/or systems?

Is your CRM definition driven by the Board of Directors and shared across the business with buy-in from all departments?

Do you have a customer segmentation model in place and measure profitability by customer segment? If not, why not? And which measures of profitability do you have in place?

CHAPTER 3

The Evolution of CRM

Definition of Marketing

CRM is simply an updated version of the definition of marketing. A bold statement perhaps but a true one. So, let's interrogate and justify.

Marketing orientated companies operating over the last 50 years would, in simple terms, define marketing as:

> *Marketing Is Identifying Consumer (Customer) Wants And Continuously Satisfying Them Profitably Within The Disciplines Of The Company's Financial Yard-Sticks.*

There are some key concepts underpinning this definition of marketing:

1. Many definitions I have seen over time use the expression of "satisfying needs." This does not fully address the personality of the consumer (customer) where their consumption behavior can be influenced by the entwined strands of emotional and functional motivations.

    NEEDS are defined as goods and services that are required as the foundation of living such as food, drink, clothing, shelter, and health care. WANTS are goods and services that are not necessary, but that are desirable or wished for. For example, one needs clothes but one may not need designer clothes.

    Needs are something you must have in order to live. On the contrary, wants are something that you wish to have to add comfort to your life and/or make you feel good; perhaps by massaging your ego. Needs represent the necessities while wants indicate desires.

This is so important in defining how products and services are designed, packaged, priced, and communicated to the consumer (customer) because it encompasses the emotional dimension of the human's complex personality.

2. The word "continuously" is central to the definition of marketing. Market research should be engaged to monitor how the wants of a company's customer universe, current and potential, are changing. This must be ongoing with the research measuring the product's (brand's) status within the context of its competitive set.

Research techniques must be sophisticated and robust to be able to interrogate the emotional and rational dimensions of customers' behavior, attitudes, and motivations to be able to predict change and quantify its impact. Tracking is essential, with results regularly and directly presented to the Board of Directors.

Even more importantly, they must act on the information and not ignore it because the ramifications of the related decisions to be taken, driven by the research findings, are perhaps seen to be too challenging and difficult to countenance.

The modern trading world is characterized by fast paced changes and shifts in buying behavior with some causal factors outside the direct control of the brand/company. For example, a new competitive entry; a change in the market dynamics due to an attitudinal shift in the customer universe (e.g., reaction to climate change), structural change (e.g., the digital age with online distribution and social media communication channels), a change in social attitudes (e.g., people get married today at the age of circa 32 years compared to 18–25 years for those born in the late 40s/50s) and the impact of the economy (e.g., unemployment and disposable income). The impact of some of these changes are immense and cannot be ignored—witness Marks & Spencer, Mothercare, Jamie Oliver's Restaurant chain, and Thomas Cook in the UK market. An example of the impact of such changes at brand level is Gillette with a double whammy. Firstly, beards became fashionable, which directly impacts the sale of replaceable blades where, one suspects, most of the profit is made. Secondly, the entry of online competition who bypass retail distribution channels by selling direct, thereby making their products universally available immediately at a very competitive price—no expense of building a sales force and a collapsed time period in reaching its target customers.

3. Financial paybacks can vary by company, from large corporates beholden to their shareholders, to private companies where a sole owner may have a different financial perspective.

4. A fundamental concept is that all employees in the company should be marketing orientated—not just a couple of offices marked "Marketing Department." This illuminates the basic truth that all employees, however specialized by function, are involved in the prime task; which is the <u>satisfaction of customer wants</u>.

The consumer (customer) is at the center of marketing and is equally the focal point of CRM. The principles of marketing have not changed. What has changed is the increased complexity a brand/company has to deal with and the laser like precision needed to market effectively. Indeed, some marketers predict that the main market differentiator in some market sectors will be customer experience instead of brand or price.

Market Changes Underpinning CRM

For many products and services, the mass marketing techniques widely practiced over the last 50 years are no longer optimal because of the radical changes in market landscapes. These, in turn, underpin the evolutionary move to CRM as the customer centric business model for managing a company competing in today's trading environment. Changes such as:

1. Audience fragmentation
   Gone are the days when demographic profiling was the be all and end all in defining target audiences.

Today, for example, in multicultural, multi-ethnic Great Britain, the population breaks down on multidimensional lines such as:

- By ethnic groups
- By sexuality
- By lifestyle
- By attitude set
- By age group with the emergence of different segments. For example, at one end of the age spectrum, post-war baby boomers in their 60s + with high levels of disposable income and a positive outlook on life. At the other end, there are a group of "career climbers" in their 20s and 30s who are highly successful and at the top income level for their life-stage.

In particular, consumers are defining themselves into identifiable groups with distinctive characteristics. Individuals self-select into groups that need to be addressed with specific benefits tailored to their particular set of wants and communicated in the optimum manner.

The answer to meet the challenges presented by audience fragmentation is customer segmentation with activities bespoke to each segment under the umbrella of the product/service overall proposition. CRM is founded on this premise.

2. Media fragmentation

The explosion in the number and type of media channels has led to greater complexity and greater difficulty for many products and services to effectively reach their target audience. In response, media agencies have developed their scientific approach to media planning with more sophisticated and advanced analytical tools and IT systems.

Targeted marketing is the order of the day, which rests at the heart of CRM (see Chapter 4, Figure 4.4).

3. More and more buying channels, as a direct result of the digital age, with a range of devices through which to research and buy products and services.

The important factor to recognize is that the customer is in charge. They have the choice and know how to exercise it. Suppliers of goods and services must recognize and accept that customers will want to do business with them from whatever channel is most convenient to them at the time. In so doing, suppliers must ensure they deliver the same standard of customer service and experience across all channels. And customers receive a personal, relevant, and seamless experience peculiar to the channel but using a consistent customer charter of handling enquiries and processing orders. Customers expect a seamless experience delivered by a single company. Everything must be unified and connected. This is the very essence of CRM.

4. The digital revolution

Transactions for goods started in the middle ages with individuals selling directly to individuals. There followed a retail evolution; primarily biased to independent traders. This culminated in a retail revolution from the 1950s onwards resulting in a very powerful and vibrant retail trade dominated by multiple operators with tremendous buying power. Their operations were progressively customer focused whilst, in parallel, becoming more operationally sophisticated through investment in computerized control and information systems and centralized distribution and stockholding. The retailer was a "king" during this phase, capturing an enormous amount of trading and customer data but not being able to universally connect purchase data to individual customers, with only partial collection through loyalty schemes.

The advent of digital online channels has turned the buying interface full circle, where customers can buy products direct and have these delivered either to their work place or home, or collected from a convenient local pick up point. Services can also be bought directly and delivered electronically. This means, the online retailer is in data paradise being able to link all purchases to individual customers and, therefore, be in a position where "knowledge is power." They can apply the data captured to analyze and use the insights generated to enhance decision making in maximizing customer development.

This is the new digital, mobile, and social world. It is dynamic and continues to disrupt the way people do business and has an impact on their expectations from a company. In this context, companies have the opportunity to use the data gathered to satisfy their customers by understanding them better as the basis to engage them—who to target, when to send communication and in which format, whether to send an offer and, if so, what type of offer and what is the most relevant content. All driven by a customer centric database giving a single customer view. This is classic CRM territory.

5. Multiplication of customer contact points. Customers expect a personal, value added, relevant contact experience, which is seamlessly delivered across all contact points and communication channels. They want to engage with you on any device, anywhere, and at any time, and expect to be consistently recognized and rewarded for their allegiance.

   Again, this can only be successfully achieved by capturing and storing all the customer data in a central customer database at the core of a CRM business model.

   Thereafter, it is up to the decision makers to harness the data from all data capture points. To profile the data to have a clear picture of customers in general, but primarily of those who contribute most to the profit and, thereby, ring fence them as VIPs. To truly understand them, their wants, and how you can best motivate and nurture an ongoing relationship with them.

   The CRM database is the engine room to support this whilst laying down the data capture protocol on the data to be captured at every customer touch point.

6. The data technical revolution

   As more and more customer data is collected, sophisticated databases and associated applied computerized techniques have developed alongside. In parallel, the cost of data storage, management, analysis, and extraction has declined dramatically making data accessible in an affordable way. This has facilitated the CRM process as a valid but tenable proposition.

Relationship Marketing

A fundamental principle embodied in CRM is to identify the most profitable customers and to retain them through building added value relationships with them.

The precursor to this approach was the process of Relationship Marketing introduced to the world of marketing in the mid-1990s and now fully embraced in CRM.

> **Relationship Marketing** used individual's consumer (customer) information to purposefully and directly manage a product's or service's customer franchise for the achievement of ongoing profit over the longer term. Its definition is:
> **"Building and promoting durable, interactive relationships between the product (service) and the individual customer, which impact on both attitudes and behavior by fully utilizing information held on a customer database."**

The essence of Relationship Marketing is in identifying a product's best prospects and converting them to lifetime loyalty. At its heart is customer retention—to keep current customers and win and convert the best target prospects to product loyalty. In so doing, to increase the level of sales revenue accounted for by loyal users as a proportion of total revenue, thereby leveraging profit.

This involves a commitment to an ongoing personalized dialogue between the customer and the product. A dialogue that builds an added value emotional bridge, which results in the customer feeling fundamentally satisfied with their product (brand) choice—not just satisfied with its functional performance.

Where this situation prevails, customers become brand advocates, which can trigger a chain reaction that the brand itself has initiated and thereafter harnessed.

By definition, Relationship Marketing is a strategic approach to marketing. It was the forerunner in one-to-one targeted marketing and is one of the pillars of CRM.

The role(s) and commercial focus of Relationship Marketing is highlighted in the following quotes:

- "Conceptually, CRM is based on relationship marketing where the primary purpose is the pursuit of profitability through customer satisfaction and loyalty while trying to maximise long-term profitability." (Zikmund, McLeod, and Gilbert 2003)

- "5% increase in customer retention boosts lifetime customer profits by 50% on average across multiple industries as well as a boost of up to 90% within specific industries e.g. insurance." (Bain & Company 2015, The story behind successful CRM, 2015, Wikipedia, accessed on April 23, 2019, https://en.wikipedia.org/wiki/Customer-realtionship_management)
- "It has been shown that the cost of soliciting new customers is seven times higher than that of retaining." (Richard and Larry 1996)
- "Relationships are not only about keeping customers over time but also about encouraging favourable attitudes toward the firm, creating customer satisfaction and generating recommendations of the firm to other potential customers." (Baharun 2008)

Some Key Thoughts to Reflect on if You Are Considering/Reviewing CRM

To what extent has your company historically operated in alignment with the Definition of Marketing? Where, if at all, has it deviated and, if so, has this negatively influenced the level of the company's profitable growth?

In particular, do you measure customer needs and wants and the extent to which they vary between customer segments? How and at which frequency do you measure customer needs/wants and the degree to which you meet them relative to other brands or companies within your competitive set?

Do you recognize the market changes influencing the progressive focus on CRM? If so, which of the factors have affected your business? Have you quantified their financial impact and put in place strategies to address them?

Are you familiar with the concept of Relationship Marketing? Do you have a Relationship Marketing program in place and, if so, which customer segments do you target? Do you measure the changes in attitudes as well as behavior resulting from the program?

What KPIs (Key Performance Indicators) do you set and report on? What payback (Return on Investment) do you achieve and over which time series?

CHAPTER 4

Developing a CRM Strategy

Overall Framework

As we have seen, CRM is a strategic approach to business management with the development of a customer centric business culture and philosophy. The central challenge is how to organize a business with the customer at its center with the singular commercial objective of optimizing customer development and profit.

Therefore, by definition, it must be led by the Board of Directors who must take direct ownership of the strategic CRM direction. It is, fundamentally, a top-down approach to profit management with the customer firmly placed at its center and, as such, involves everyone in the business. The customer is no longer the sole province of sales or marketing or customer service. It embraces everyone and all of the company's processes, technologies, and most importantly, its staff must be aligned to support and deliver the CRM objectives. It must be organizationally structured to effectively and efficiently manage all aspects of CRM but, critically, all staff must be imbued with a customer facing ethos with an outward looking focus on placing the customer first.

Arguably, a company's internal stakeholders are just as important in successfully implementing a CRM strategy as the customers themselves!

Given a CRM strategic vision and program is for the long haul, a robust, disciplined, structured approach **must** be adopted with a number of steps undertaken to develop and implement a CRM strategy.

However, in doing so, we must acknowledge that although CRM principles are common to all businesses, the CRM operational model will vary according to the type of business; whether the company sells directly to the end user or markets their product/service through intermediaries to reach the ultimate end user. For the latter, there are two basic types of businesses to which CRM applies:

A. The primary supplier of the product or service. This company has two "customer" interfaces to account for in the development of a CRM strategy:
   • The intermediaries (e.g., bricks and mortar retailers, online retailers, wholesalers, distributors, agents) who are their trading partners (customers), and who they invoice and service.
   • The end users of their products or services. For example, consumers for B2C companies or professional tradesmen for home related products.
B. The intermediaries whose customers are the end users of the products or services they are selling.

From the primary supplier's perspective, the complexities to take on board escalate according to the concentration of power and the CRM strategies (see the following Tesco case study in this chapter) adopted by the major players in the distribution channels for their products.

For example, this is particularly acute for "Fast Moving Consumer Goods" (FMCG) producers marketing products through grocery retail channels:

A revolution of change was accelerated from the 1980s and continues through to the present day with the progressive move toward online businesses. Retailers' businesses are increasingly customer (shopper) focused whilst, in parallel, more operationally sophisticated through investment in computerized IT systems and the supply chain with centralized distribution and stockholding. More importantly, their data knowledge bank of customer behavior and profile is expansive.

Retailers, previously informed and educated and in some cases perhaps even dictated to by suppliers, are now in a more powerful position than ever before; to the extent that they are not only controlling whether a product will be presented to the consumer, they are deciding how it will be merchandised to best suit their own needs. Now, many suppliers are no longer in a position to control or, indeed, influence how their products should be merchandised and sold at the point of purchase.

There is also a parallel in how a product is promoted to the consumer. A supplier is often restricted to participating in the retailer's own promotional platform or not at all. However, the promotional formats and associated promotion mechanics may be incompatible with both the brand's consumer objectives and its brand values.

For many suppliers, this presents a marketing conundrum. The point of sale is an important point of contact between the brand and consumer, and influence is being diluted on the conditions under which direct contact with the consumer is made.

In this scenario, it is easy to see the relevance and value of managing a supplier's business through a CRM business model. It is vital that a partnership approach is adopted with retail customers that fully recognizes and takes account of their needs and operational modus operandi.

From the above, it is readily apparent that "one size does not fit all" when applied to companies developing and implementing a CRM strategy. In this respect, I set out the general steps involved and encourage individual companies to adapt and adopt those that apply to them. I translate this into some practical guidelines by illustrating CRM in action through two case studies in the following section in this chapter.

CRM operates at both company and brand levels. We have used "brand" as the simple reference in our guideline notes but interpret this as including "company" where it is featured.

The steps involved are recommended as follows:

Step 1

The start point is to understand where your brand sits in its market sector among its competitive set. This is absolutely fundamental and there should be no excuse based on the required data not being available. If data is not available through external data panels, surveys should be conducted to collect and collate the required data.

The analysis should be conducted on three major dimensions:

1. Build an in-depth profile of the target customer (recognizing that primary suppliers selling products/services through intermediaries have two target audiences) in overall terms and by segment (see section "2" below) to understand any differences that should be

incorporated into the strategic planning. An outline guide to a check list is given below:

- Their characteristics. For B2C companies, for example, covering their demographics, geodemographics, lifestyle, their general attitude set, and so on.
- Their needs and wants, covering both functional and emotional dimensions, and motivations.
- Identify what drives and underpins their purchasing behavior for the sector and their perceptions of the competing brands operating in the sector and highlighting any differences.
- Identify any subset requiring special focus and build a particularly robust profile. For example, a loyal heavy user group who account for a disproportionate share of profit relative to the size of their customer universe. These will constitute the "best customer" segment.

2. Conduct a strenuous financial audit by deconstructing the brand's revenue base into its different usage behavioral segments from two perspectives:

a. Firstly, to identify the brand's sources of revenue and profit from its current customer base segregated into their purchase value segments.

On a simple one-dimensional level, it will quantify how customers vary in their contribution to revenue and profit. Figure 4.1 illustrates how the profile can vary by customer segment in their share of customers, revenue, and profit.

b. Secondly, to assess the brand's relative position within its market sector.

The analysis exercise evaluates the brand's market status by building a three dimensional model on the axes of customer loyalty (share of wallet), purchase behavior for the category, and attitudes toward the brand and category. The analysis pinpoints which customer groups are most important to the brand's current and future financial health whilst identifying the threats and opportunities. Above all, it demonstrates that **"while all customers are equal, some are more equal than others."**

The analysis results in a model that is best described as the "BRAND EQUITY MATRIX."

% of customers, revenue, and profit

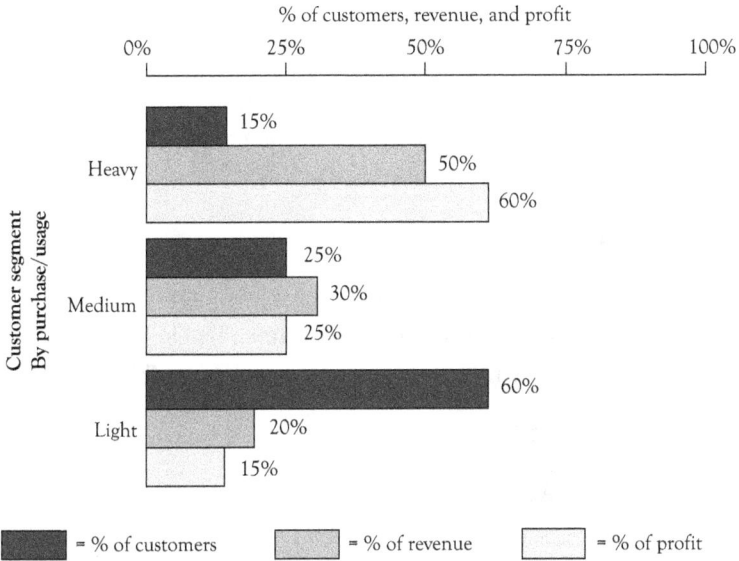

Figure 4.1 **Customer segment by volume of annual purchases**

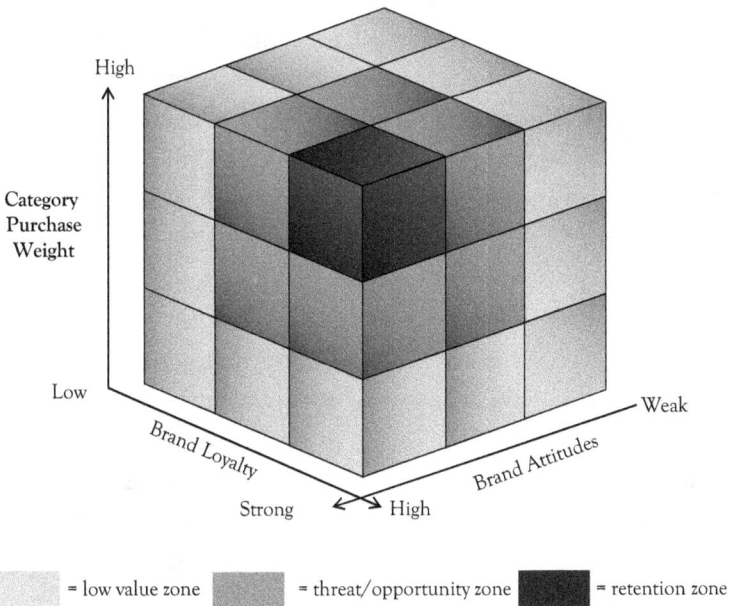

Figure 4.2 **The brand equity matrix**

A simple model is depicted in Figure 4.2 in which each axis has three criteria resulting in a total of 27 cells.

It will highlight which clusters are of greater importance to the brand's equity than others, which customers are of most value, and which are most susceptible to being lost.

In the matrix there are three main cluster zones:

- The "RETENTION" zone in which the most valuable customers will reside. Their potential lifetime value to the brand will be extremely high relative to the other zones. This is the top priority segment to retain and develop as brand ambassadors.
- The "THREAT/OPPORTUNITY" zone, which presents the main risks and gains area where customers buy from a brand portfolio with many buying one particular brand "most often." This will comprise a mix of customers containing, for example, customers of only medium loyalty but with positive attitudes and healthy category value. The "attitude" dimension enhances the ability to target by those belonging to either the "threats" or "opportunities" classifications.
- The "LOW VALUE" zone, which contributes the least amount of brand revenue either because they have low category value and/or because they are low brand loyalists who may be promiscuous category buyers. They may have a range of attitudes toward the brand from positive to negative.

Examining the behavior of existing customers is also the optimal way of defining new target customer groups who are category buyers but, currently, non-brand buyers. The value of those customers can equally be estimated.

In essence, this constitutes the brand's strategic customer centric model. The data can be aggregated as depicted in Table 4.1, which provides a simple illustration of the analysis output with each segment in the matrix populated with the data.

Table 4.1 *Category profile of brand buyers*

CUSTOMER LOYALTY AND ATTITUDES	NUMBER OF TOTAL BRAND BUYERS				ANNUAL VALUE OF TOTAL BRAND BUYERS			
	CATEGORY PURCHASE WEIGHT				CATEGORY PURCHASE WEIGHT			
	HEAVY	MEDIUM	LIGHT	TOTAL	HEAVY	MEDIUM	LIGHT	TOTAL
100% LOYAL								
Stable								
Susceptible								
70–99% LOYAL								
Stable								
Susceptible								
31–69% LOYAL								
Susceptible								
Promiscuous								
1–30% LOYAL								
0% LOYAL								
TOTAL								

DEFINITIONS

100% LOYAL   = "SOLUS BRAND BUYERS"
70–99% LOYAL = "MOST OFTEN BUYERS", where the brand is the preferred choice
31–69% LOYAL = "SOMETIMES BUYERS", where the brand features in a basket of brands
1–30% LOYAL = Buy brand probably only on promotion or, for an FMCG brand, when their preferred brand is "out of stock"
0% LOYAL   = Category buyers who are non-brand buyers
STABLE   = A positive attitude toward the brand and they are the least likely to brand switch
SUSCEPTIBLE = They do not have a strong relationship with the brand and are open to considering competing brand propositions
PROMISCUOUS = Buy from a portfolio of brands with their brand selection mainly determined by promotion offers

Note: there should be two computations of annual value: one based on the total category spend and the other based on the spend on the brand. For the latter, spend for the "0% loyal" segment will obviously be zero.

The exercise results in a quantified set of existing and potential new customers and knowing the value and loyalty status and potential of each loyalty group. From this, for example, we are able to:

- Quantify opportunities for revenue growth through recruiting new customers and/or increasing customer loyalty and, for both, the ability to identify the target customer profiles.
- Identify the opportunities and threats, particularly among the semi-loyal segments, and what is required to realize the opportunities and to negate the threats.
- Identify the brand's strengths and weaknesses relative to the competing brands and understand which brand(s) offer the main threat and why.
- Quantify the contribution and related importance of a loyal customer group to revenue by purchase value category. In so doing, to profile the loyalty segments as the foundation on which to develop customer related programs tailored to their particular set of needs and wants.
- Identify any threats to category growth and the degree to which they can be confronted and nullified. For example, a move to eating at home using takeaway catering services and diluting the frequency of eating out.

The model provides the strategic framework from which to set objectives with priorities defined, together with determining the allocation of funds and resources. Given the strategic nature of the model, it should be updated on a fixed time cycle with the time lapse dependent on the purchase frequency for the sector (e.g., from every year through to a 5-year cycle) and any unforeseen significant strategic competitive initiative.

The pivotal thought around segmentation is summarized by Malthouse and Mulhern: "The combination of knowledge about how consumers feel about a brand with knowledge about the financial value of those consumers provides organisations with the ability to strategically form segments and develop branding strategy." (Malthouse and Mulhern 2007)

3. There is a primary need to manage the brand based on data regularly captured comprising behavioral data and personal characteristics, whilst being fully cognizant of and loyal to the pursuit of the strategic goals.

Hence, an important step is to evolve the strategic model into an ongoing operational model as the reference for purposefully managing and developing the customer consistent with the strategic framework.

To achieve this, a customer segmentation model is built in which the brand is deconstructed into its different user groups on the dimensions of recency, frequency, and value (RFV) as shown in Figure 4.3.

The segmentation model enables the annual customer development and communications budget to be allocated against specific objectives and customer segments. Budgets can also be allocated in direct relation to the expected return or danger of customer loss.

The operational model runs in parallel with the strategic changes required by the findings of the strategic financial and marketing audits.

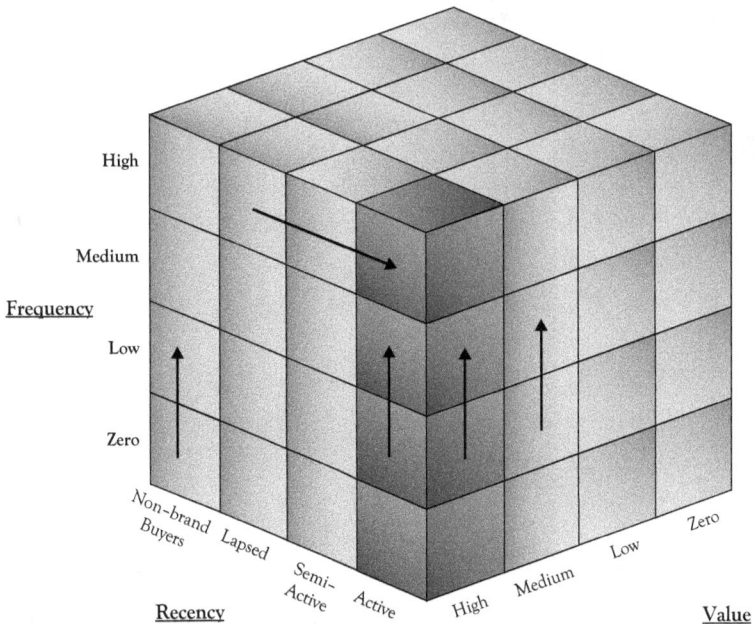

Figure 4.3 Customer segmentation model

Targeting customers residing in each segment is enhanced by building customer pen profiles, which leverages communication effectiveness and efficiency. This uses the two strands of data captured:

- Behavioral data comprising their purchase history, responses to any communication campaigns, and redemption of any promotion offers.
- Personal characteristics captured, which is dependent on the data capture protocols used. For B2C consumers, for example, it should, at a minimum, embrace postcode (as the reference for geodemographic profiling), age, gender, and presence of children.

Relevant information should be tagged to each individual on the database to be used to direct and enhance the effectiveness of communication campaigns—what to say, to whom, and when. Campaigns can then be built using multivariable selection criteria based on the data held by segment. In so doing, pen portraits should be built to give target profiles to guide communication tone, copy style, creativity, and content together with promotion incentives.

The information tagged should ideally be structured in sections to aid user group understanding and simplify data extraction and applications such as:

A. Section 1: Housing data used to develop personal profiles. In B2B, this will cover company profiles and those of the primary and secondary decision makers.
B. Section 2: Holding behavioral data.

This approach is illustrated below using a casual dining restaurant group as the reference with their customer database primarily populated by members of their Loyalty Club:

Section 1: Personal Profile

In the first instance, the customer database was geodemographically matched against the GB (Great Britain) geodemographic universe to analyze the degree to which the customer profile was skewed. The opportunity for geodemographic groups to be amalgamated into communication clusters based on the common characteristics was an important analysis output. Six key geodemographic clusters were identified, which accounted for over 80 percent of revenue. Pen profiles could then be built with cluster names to make them easy to remember (e.g., Golden Oldies) using the following parameters:

- Age
- Gender
- Occupation
- Home status
- Family: couple, single, children, and so on
- Lifestyle portrait covering finances, internet usage, social media usage, other digital applications usage, media consumption, eating out, hobbies and interests, holidays and so on
- General attitudes

Section 2: Behavior Profile

Based on the data captured, the following could be used as inputs in developing a behavior profile at the individual customer level:

- Daypart for restaurant visits: Breakfast, lunch, dinner
- Weekday versus weekend visits
- Number of covers by meal by daypart
- Meals taken with/without alcohol by daypart
- Meals taken with/without children: defined by selections off the children's menu, by daypart
- Transaction value by meal by daypart
- Basket analysis of meal composition: starter/main/dessert/ beverages (alcoholic and non-alcoholic)
- Eating out on special occasion days: Valentine's Day, Mother's Day, Easter, Bank Holidays, Father's Day, Christmas
- Frequency of eating out in restaurants, including pub restaurants, as a measure of potential with frequency scales provided
- Where customers eat out by frequency; five venue descriptors and four options on the frequency scale provided

- Participation in the loyalty program. For example, where points are involved—points earned and points redeemed by date by outlet
- Responses to promotion activities

The data captured and attached to all individual residents in the database can be used to tailor relevant communication to the different clusters within each segment, which enables engagement levels to be maximized which, in turn, supports the customer objectives being met.

It provides a high grade targeting tool with data used as a primary asset in delivering highly focused, value added, and motivating communication.

Step 2

Set formal, quantified customer objectives. Define strategic goals of business engagement with current and potential future customers to maximize long-term sales and profit. The output from the previous step is the data reference for setting the objectives and laying down priorities in ranking order.

Step 3

Assess the company's organizational capabilities and readiness to support the customer objectives. Whether it has the technology, human resources, processes, and appropriate skills to support and meet the defined goals?

This is an absolutely mission critical exercise and, as such, must be conducted in the most disciplined, robust, honest, and realistic manner with zero tolerance for any "fudges." It must be supervised by a senior management team comprising the heads of all relevant departmental functions with a formal, written report prepared and presented to the Board for discussion and sign off. The key output will be a critical path setting down the actions and timings to align the company's resources behind the strategic plan. This will include all the relevant costs: investment and operational.

"In order to generate intelligence and disseminate it throughout the organisation, a company must have the right staff, economic resources

and specific know-how, as well as the appropriate technological tools."
(Cambra-Fierro, Centeno, Olavarria, and Vasquez-Carrasco 2017)

Some of the central considerations are outlined below.

Technology

A primary factor driving CRM success is the functionality and user acceptance of the technology required to build customer knowledge and manage customer interactions.

This covers all the aspects of technology required to support the CRM
strategy—information systems, CRM software, sales force automation,
data warehouse, data mining, help desk, internet interface, call centers,
and so on.

IT capability is obviously a given. The other three key factors are as
follows:

a. The commercial development of CRM software drives and enables
   CRM as a business strategy. Software packages offer a comprehensive set of technologies for managing relationships with current and
   potential customers and business partners across sales, marketing,
   and customer service, covering all the touch points with the customers, regardless of the communication channel.

   Such software is primarily sourced through external third parties either through bespoke solutions or proprietary systems with
   the solution determined by meeting the written functional specification laying down the company's CRM software needs.

b. The most important asset in determining the successful outcome of
   CRM is the knowledge the company possesses. Knowledge management is the systems and processes deployed in managing (e.g.,
   capturing, storing, retrieving, and applying data) and making available the intelligence and insight generated from the data resident
   in the organization. In so doing, to apply and refine knowledge
   management systems in order to get optimal value added knowledge for themselves and their customers. The systems' specification
   for capturing, building, managing, and applying customer data is a
   pivotal requirement of CRM planning.

c. Knowledge is power and it is directly related to the data captured, stored, and applied. It is therefore imperative to:

- Lay down the customer data specification of the data required and where and how it can be obtained
- Audit all the current data capture points to specify the data captured. Identify gaps and how to fill them resulting in an updated data capture protocol to be applied and tailored to each data capture point
- Audit data transfer processes, where data sets are housed and data application tools used. In so doing, identify areas for improvement assessed against the criteria of, for example, data security (compliance with the GDPR in the UK); data accessibility by all the user groups; automatic data transfer from all the data capture points into a central customer data warehouse; data analytical tools
- Develop a comprehensive database/data specification with the functionality to deliver the required data management solution

Process

A central theme of a CRM strategy is to aim to create and satisfy a long-term relationship with target customers. As such, it is essential to analyze the processes that in any way involve and impact interactions with customers, which mainly comprise marketing, sales, and customer services functions.

In this context, there are two central requirements, which must be fully interrogated with the solution specified:

A. CRM success is contingent upon a company's ability to detect and respond to evolving customer needs, wants, and preferences. The processes need to be set to deliver this.

B. Customer data captured must be securely stored and processed and be fully compliant with, in the UK, the GDPR. This requires a comprehensive, formal process specification to be drawn up.

The Human Factor

The human factor is obviously crucial in a company handling and managing external customer relationships in a professional and courteous manner. To have an ongoing mutually beneficial, stable customer relationship, a company must be cognizant of four key aspects:

- Know how the customer defines value
- Provide ongoing satisfaction according to the wants and value standards of the customer
- Constantly strive toward customer retention and loyalty
- To provide a professional service at each point of customer contact in a customer friendly manner that reflects the way you would like to be treated yourself

To fully take account of these and delivering CRM, all levels of the organization must be aligned toward favoring and supporting customer relationships with a total commitment to a customer centric focus. This should take on board the following:

A. The change in culture required by the company's staff. For example, switching from a product centric approach to a customer centric approach requires a change in attitude and ethos within the organization.

   The degree to which a company's culture is integrated and aligned with its strategic CRM objectives, goals, and expected outcomes will positively impact the overall organizational performance. A CRM driven organization must aim all its efforts at managing and satisfying customer wants profitably. Creating, delivering, and communicating customer value more effectively than their competitors. This will not be achieved unless everyone in the organization is singing off the same customer focused hymn sheet.

B. The role played by employees in successfully establishing a customer relationship is a pre-requisite to, in turn, generate customer loyalty and translate it into profit. Therefore, employee retention becomes just as important as customer retention. The longer the employee feels motivated and satisfied, the higher the commitment level to the company to, in turn, apply "best practice" skills in customer management and relationship building.

C. The degree of commitment and participation in the CRM strategic process on the part of those in high management positions is another critical factor. CRM has to be an "inclusive" philosophy with all senior management fully on board and signing up to the direction of travel.

Defining the optimal organizational structure and culture to deliver CRM and how to move toward this is probably the most challenging aspect of installing a CRM strategy. As such, it is vital that a blueprint is developed and devotedly followed to cross the finishing line.

With this in mind, it is worth remembering that the following factors are often cited as reasons why a CRM strategy was not successfully implemented:

- The Board was not unified in following the CRM strategic path, which compromised all the aspects of CRM
- Not fully using company resources to obtain the data to build customer profiles because they thought they already knew the customer
- Ignoring system integration and organizational, cultural importance believing that just a CRM software package was enough
- Inefficient communication between departments involved in the various CRM processes
- Lack of metrics capable of measuring and understanding CRM's commercial benefits and the financial impact of changes within the company

Step 4

Align the organization behind the goals

From the inputs above, set clear desired, quantified commercial results of CRM and identify the steps to achieve the vision. The strategy to achieve the objectives should cover the following:

- Customer proposition and differential benefits
- Vision

- Customer segmentation
- Customer experience
- Organizational structure and culture
- Processes
- Customer data
- Technology
- Metrics

Step 5

Customer engagement sits at the center of customer development. Building a relationship bridge between the customer and the brand provides the best opportunity to develop customer loyalty.

This can only be realistically achieved if the brand's proposition is, on the one hand, relevant in addressing and meeting customer wants and, on the other hand, is readily understood by customers through communication.

As such, it is essential to define the brand's benefits in meeting customer wants (i.e., why should customers buy your brand in preference to other brands) and to translate them into a brand positioning statement. This should be understood across the company and by all the external communication agencies employed by the company. It is, in essence, the brand's bible and is one of the brand's main building blocks.

Step 6

Execute CRM program with each phase clearly demarcated.

Step 7

Measure program effectiveness on an ongoing basis and implement any corrective actions required. Monitor key metrics measuring progress toward the commercial objectives with regular, formal reporting to the Board.

Case Studies

The principles of CRM can be applied at total company or individual brand levels. We provide a case study for each to give a practical illustration of CRM.

In both cases, the numbers provided in the models are for directional purposes based on research, personal judgment, assumptions, and interpretation.

The accompanying comments are based on a combination of background research, personal experience, and observation and should therefore be viewed as opinions.

TESCO*

Background

Tesco is a multiple supermarket retailer in the UK. In the 1970s, it was the number 2 brand in its market sector. By 2012, it was the clear brand leader, had expanded internationally, and became the third largest global retailer after Walmart in the United States and Carrefour in France.

The case study traces how it transformed itself into "best and top in class" and became the benchmark model for the UK retail industry.

By the 1970s, Tesco was building a national network of stores to cover the whole of the UK under the leadership of Jack Cohen (later to become Sir Jack Cohen). The central platform of their success was founded on the "Pile 'em high, sell 'em cheap" formula imported from the United States.

This, however, is only a headline statement and masks the innovation and forward thinking actions underpinning the growth Tesco experienced. Jack Cohen, arguably, understood what worked for the mass market and Tesco could exploit this for its own commercial benefits. Some examples were:

- There was an in-built philosophy that shops should be owned. To this end, a national network was developed from the 1950s; primarily through acquisition.
- Diversification with non-food items introduced in the 1960s. "Home n Wear" departments were located in larger stores to carry higher margin clothing and household merchandise.
- Tesco was the first adopter of a loyalty scheme through Green Shield stamps in 1963.
- They opened their first petrol stations in 1974 and became the UK's largest independent petrol retailer.

However, the market was changing from the early 1970s leaving the company with slim margins and a serious image problem.

Ian MacLaurin (later to become Baron MacLaurin of Knebworth) succeeded Jack Cohen in 1973 as CEO, which was the catalyst for a strategic review.

CRM Audit – The Start Point

Using our Brand Equity model as a guide, the review would have potentially drawn the following insights:

a. Loyalty Dimension

Tesco, at the time, had a low "share of wallet" among its grocery shoppers, at approximately 35 percent, indicating that shoppers were not completely satisfied with the Tesco grocery shopping offering.

The potential prize by increasing loyalty among its existing shoppers was enormous.

This is illustrated in the model below; largely based on the 1998 data assumptions with the key commercial objective to increase "share of wallet" from 35 percent to 55 percent. The latter equates to Tesco being, on average, the preferred brand choice among its shoppers. Thus:

- Total average household expenditure on food and drink (alcoholic and non-alcoholic) for in-home consumption per annum = £3966
- Number of GB households = 23,434,900
- Tesco household penetration = 44 percent = 10,311,356 households
- Maximum annual spend by Tesco shoppers: 10,311,356 homes x £3966 = £40,894,837,896
- Increase "share of wallet" from 35 percent to 55 percent:
- £40,894,837,896 x 0.55 = £22,492,160,843
- £40,894,837,896 x 0.35 = £14,313,193, 264
- Incremental potential annual gain = £8,178,967, 579

Focusing on developing customer loyalty and customer retention would be identified as a key commercial objective.

b. <u>Category Purchase Weight Dimension</u>

The rump of Tesco shoppers were in the lower social classes with associated lower spend per household but, more importantly, expenditure biased toward lower margin products. The profile was therefore skewed toward the "medium" category purchase weight segment.

Hence, acquisition of new, higher spend households and converting them into loyal customers would be identified as a key strategic objective.

The potential financial gain is substantial as measured by the **customer lifetime value,** which, on average, equates to £95,000 per person. Hence, the earlier a target customer is recruited in their adult lifecycle, the greater the gain.

c. <u>Attitude Dimension</u>

Attitudes toward and perceptions of Tesco were generally graded as unfavorable on the following dimensions:

1. Poor shopping experience:
   - Narrow aisles
   - Poor layout
   - Long queues
   - Poor store access given the majority were smaller (relative to today) high street based units
   - Not seen to be pristinely clean
   - Store clutter with displays scattered all over the store
2. Fresh produce offering not viewed as top quality
3. Not perceived to be a high quality brand; particularly by Sainsbury's shoppers, Sainsbury's being the number 1 brand in Great Britain at the time with their strength biased toward London and the South East with a higher income/social class shopper profile. In contrast, Tesco had a more down-market, "cheap and cheerful" image.

It was clearly evident that, first and foremost, the "CORE PRODUCT" had to be radically improved and the brand repositioned if Tesco was to engage a wider shopper audience whilst also cementing customer loyalty.

CRM *Strategy*

Fundamentally, Ian MacLaurin progressively moved the organization from a buying led, operations centric business to a customer centric model in which a "customer first" culture pervaded the company.

The primary motivation for change was a commercial one to improve the financial performance of the company and maximize shareholder value. The route to deliver this was to drive expansion to achieve the number 1 brand status in the grocery market and the key to achieve this was to adopt a strategy rooted in CRM principles and practices.

The challenge was to comprehensively modernize Tesco and make it an "aspirational mass retailer." This was accomplished in phases over a 30+ year journey.

Phase 1: Improve the "core product" and make it fit for purpose
As marketers, we all know that the "product" is the hero in the marketing equation. We can try every trick in the book to get the customer to repeat but will not be successful if the "Trial" experience disappoints and does not meet expectations and the standards required.

In Tesco's case, the actions taken to improve the shopper experience and reposition the brand on a quality platform covered the following:

A. Discontinued Green Shield Trading Stamps and launched "Operation Checkout," which reduced prices by between 3 and 26 percent across 1,500 food items. This addressed two issues: firstly that Tesco was perceived as expensive by many shoppers at the time and, secondly, Green Shield Stamps were progressively seen as yesterday's gimmick and contributed to Tesco's down-market image.

B. Closed 500 unprofitable, smaller stores.

C. Extensively upgraded and enlarged others.

D. Customer focused product development incorporating rigorous testing. This initially manifested itself through:
   - The introduction of own label
   - Introduction of the "Value Range" in 1993 recognizing that some sections of society were under the financial cosh stemming from the performance of the economy

E. Putting heavy investment in the supply chain to maximize efficiency, minimize "out of stock" in store and derive optimal benefit from the advent of the bar code system. Distribution systems were computerized and centralized which translated into enormous cost savings. Hitherto stockholding, many supplier deliveries and, to a degree, buying decisions were made at local store level.

F. Customer focused store development. More than most, Tesco talked to prospective customers as it built and fitted stores. They included "meet the public" sessions as well as surveys. Stores were built for public tastes. They prioritized the development of large out-of-town stores where parking was convenient, shopper selection of goods broad and where a higher volume of business could be generated at increased margins while reducing overheads. Stores were modern, clean, with wide aisles, improved layouts and lots of tills.

- Growth was fueled by the increase in the number of working women who no longer had the time or inclination to shop by foot at small outlets—butchers, greengrocers, and fishmongers. Their needs were further met by the opening of the first 24 hour store.

- The property portfolio was huge with Tesco developers working in partnership with local planning authorities. The focal point for development was Sainsbury's heartland in middle class England, which was the target bullseye for expansion of the customer base.

G. Dramatically upped their game in the supply and presentation in-store of fresh produce. The radical improvements made to the supply chain efficiency played a significant role in facilitating this.

H. Sainsbury's customer proposition was summarized in the slogan "Good food costs less." Tesco trumped this when in 1992 (carefully staged after many of the store improvements had been made) they introduced "Every Little Helps." This attracted 1.3 million new customers between 1993 and 1995 and helped Tesco reposition itself from being a down-market, high volume, low-cost retailer to one designed to appeal to and attract a range of social groups.

I. New stores and refurbished ones incorporated heavy investment in the most up-to-date and extensive chilled and freezer cabinets. Once again, this was fully in tune with customer lifestyle trends and could accommodate high margin new product development in chilled products.

J. Having pioneered and spearheaded the development of out-of-town shopping centers, Tesco headed back into town "high streets" with the introduction of small convenience stores called "Tesco Metro" as a sub-brand. This was followed by further brand extensions fitted to alternative store formats that met different sets of customer needs: "Tesco Express" located on garage forecourts and "Tesco Extra" as their superstore, offering their most comprehensive range of food and non-food items.

K. The "One in Front" campaign launched in 1994 in which a new till was opened whenever a checkout line exceeded two trolleys.

Phase 2: Changing gear to a higher level of customer focus
The ultimate challenge was how to build and cement individual customer relationships as the foundation on which to achieve its customer loyalty ("share of wallet") objectives.

The answer: **THE BIRTH OF TESCO CLUBCARD IN 1995.**

This was a loyalty scheme built for the age of computerized research. There were two strands to the thinking behind Tesco Clubcard:

- How to measure individual behavior given it was not practical to stick a barcode on a customer's forehead so they would be recognized when they entered the store?
- How to reward individual behavior? Following testing, a 1 percent loyalty bonus (1 point for every £ spent over £5) was enough and provided flexibility to add promotions and giveaways.

It was the first supermarket loyalty card, which, over time, irreversibly changed the marketing landscape of retailers, brands, and customers.

Tesco Clubcard enabled Tesco to capture raw data on what people were buying and turn it into profitable information. With the Clubcard, Tesco totally understood **INFORMATION IS POWER.** It was pivotal in understanding customers and enabled a series of innovations and developments to follow on the back of it.

From the data captured, they gathered fundamental knowledge on personal and shopping profiles:

- Who they were
- Where they lived
- Which Tesco stores they shopped in
- When they shopped
- How much they spent
- Which departments they shopped in

The data highlighted the importance of frequency. Before, from in-store observations, the belief was that the key shopper was a **mother with 2 children** struggling around the store with an overflowing trolley. In reality, an older lady with a basket came in five times a week buying higher margin products generating a higher profit than the mother with 2 children who shopped once a month.

The introduction of Tesco Clubcard and the knowledge gathered spawned the following benefits:

A. Customer focused ranging. It enabled Tesco to be much better, much faster at ranging at store level for the local audience. Tailoring ranging to a store's catchment area profile taking account of ethnicity and nationality. And the bigger Tesco got, the broader its audience became, so the better Tesco could understand how that audience varied by location was a distinct competitive advantage.

B. It underpinned customer focused product development. For example, it was the foundation on which "Tesco Finest" (a superior quality own label range) was launched aimed at more aspirational, higher income customers. It quickly became a really significant brand and directly attacked Marks & Spencer's strength in ready meals; Marks & Spencer being the premier own label quality reference at the time in Great Britain.

C. It enabled customer segments with particular characteristics to be identified and their relationship nurtured by developing innovative ideas tailored to their needs. For example, the introduction of Tesco Baby Club, Wine Club, and Pet Club.

D. It provided a customer base to which new products could be marketed. For example:
  • Tesco Personal Finance launched in 1997 with a Visa Card and a range of insurance products.
  • Tesco.com launched in 2000 with 20,000 members visiting the site every month in the first year.

E. Market research turnaround on new products was cut from months to weeks and brands could see early on whether new products should be rolled out nationwide.

F. The card generated significantly increased traffic from new and repeat customers enabling customers to experience a modernized, rejuvenated Tesco shopper experience that met their customer wants.

Normal promotions are often asking people to swap brands but Tesco Clubcard was rewarding customers on their normal shops in a new store environment and a product offering that was very much to their liking.

First and foremost, it was a big thank you and that thank you was money off, which led to shoppers revisiting the store, which led to millions and millions of pounds extra revenue. And occasionally, they put an extra item in their basket, which translated into a further revenue boost.

This worked incredibly well because the concept of "the more you spend, the more you get" was in tune with a high regular frequency of shopping. Moreover, the perception of scale was enhanced by the use of Tesco Clubcard partner companies, which facilitated the impression of a multiplier effect.

G. The databank became an asset in its own right, which enabled Tesco to leverage new income streams from suppliers by giving them access to the customer base through Tesco. Tesco would never share customer data with third parties but it would communicate to the database on behalf of a brand using scientifically based selection criteria. In this regard, Tesco was very "picky" on the brands it partnered.

The response rates on promotions to Tesco Clubcard holders was really high; often in a range of 40–60 percent. The response rate was 10 times higher through the Tesco Clubcard medium compared to any other promotion.

H. It was a true loyalty program. In addition to the overall points reward system, customers received coupon incentives in their quarterly statements on brands that they normally bought. This was another way of promoting loyalty. In this context, over 900 customer segments were created based on common shopping behavior characteristics.

I. Direct Marketing was initially used as the main communication channel to the customer database covering both the quarterly statement and tactical mailings. Direct Marketing has continued to be a main communication channel since the program was launched in 1995 and stands out as an exception in the digital age. Judgmentally, this is purposefully done for two main reasons:

- It enhances engagement with all the communication being personalized. Personalization through postal communication has far more emotional connection than through digital applications. This is one of the primary factors in delivering exceptional response rates.
- Offers are personalized with a range of coupons/vouchers contained in the quarterly statement redeemed against varying date lines. These are a form of "currency," which are often kept in a purse or wallet making redemption "top of mind" at the point of purchase. Once again, an example of clear thinking.

Results

a. It ratcheted up its "share of wallet" proportion in excess of its initial horizon. This, in all probability, generated an incremental annual revenue gain in excess of £8 billion.

b. It increased its household penetration thereby generating incremental revenue from newly acquired customers.

The potential commercial benefits from this are illustrated in the model below:

- Percentage of GB households using Tesco as their main shop: 20.8 percent in 1993 and 28 percent in 2003

- Number of GB households: 22,225,000 in 1993 and 24,400,000 in 2003
- Number of households using Tesco as their main shop: 4,622,800 in 1993 and 6,832,000 in 2003
- Incremental gain in Tesco households = 2,209,000
- Incremental gain in spend potential per annum: 2,209,200 x £3966 spend per household = £8.8 billion.

c. As a result of the achievements mentioned in (a) and (b) above, Tesco overtook Sainsbury's as the brand leader in the grocery market in 1996 and accelerated away.

Its financial performance was exemplary and dynamic:

	Turnover	Profit
1998	£16.45bn	£760mn
2003	£26.33bn	£1.36bn
2008	£47.29bn	£2.8bn
2013	£64.83bn	£3.55bn

By 1999, it grew in share to 19 percent compared to Sainsbury's at 14.4 percent. By 2005, its share grew to over 30 percent reaching a peak of 30.6 percent in 2011.

For a comparison relevant to the time, Tesco did to Sainsbury's what New Labour, under Tony Blair, did to the Tories in UK politics in the late 1990s. It hijacked its ideas, added value, and stole the hearts of middle England.

Today, there are 16.5 million Tesco Clubcard users.

d. The establishment of the core Tesco brand and its credentials and trust with consumers enabled it to extend the brand into other sectors generating new income streams.

Conclusions

Tesco transformed itself into a customer centric business with a customer focused culture. To quote Amazon's Mantra "Start with the customer and work backwards." Understand your customers, anticipate their needs and wants and give them what they will value. Tesco did this in spades in the 35 year period from 1973.

They developed a CRM philosophy with the cornerstones being:

- Moved to a customer centric business from a buying centric business.
- Translated this internally with the Company's proposition expressed as "The Tesco Way" describing the company's core purposes, values, principles, and goals. This reinforced the focal shift to people: both customers and employees.
- Tesco's mission was to create value for their customers, to earn their lifetime value delivered through two themes:
  - No one tries harder than we do for our customers
  - We treat people the way we like to be treated

The Commercial Output Speaks for Itself

*(Born, Left on the shelf, thanks to Tesco, Daily Telegraph, June 3, 1999), (Clark and Szu Ping Chan, History of Tesco: The rise of Britain's Biggest Supermarket, Telegraph, October 4, 2013, accessed December 12, 2019), (Corporate Watch, Tesco Company Profile, October 14, 2004, accessed December 17, 2019), (Molly Fleming, We have to make sure it didn't fall on its arse: How Tesco revolutionised loyalty with Clubcard, Marketing Week, Mach, 2013), (Hassan and Parves 2013), (Nicole Martin, Shoppers find more choice elsewhere, Daily Telegraph, June 3, 1999), (Kate Rankine, Sainsbury's cuts 1,000 jobs as profits falter, Daily Telegraph, June 3, 1999), (Tesco plc, Annual reports and Accounts), (Wikipedia, s.v. "Tesco", accessed December 12, 2019, https://en.wikiprdia.org/wiki/Tesco), (Denise Winterman, Tesco: How one supermarket came to dominate, BBC News Magazine, September 9, 2013, accessed December 17, 2019)

Malt Whisky Brand

This case study is based on a premium brand in the Great Britain Malt Whisky market.

Background

A segmentation study was conducted using an external data panel (Target Group Index – TGI) to evaluate the source of volume and profit across consumer segments and, in so doing, to determine the most appropriate marketing strategy going forward. The principal findings were:

1. The market was highly skewed toward a very heavy user group as shown in Table 4.2:

Table 4.2 Market segmentation by volume of annual purchases

	% of Drinkers	% of Volume	Average Bottles per Drinker per year
User Segment: Category Usage			
Super Heavy	2.4	30.8	18.4
Heavy	21.6	47.1	3.2
Super Heavy/Heavy Combined	24.0	77.9	4.7
Medium	25.2	13.2	0.8
Light	50.8	8.9	0.3
Total	100	100	1.45

The segmentation dynamics encouraged a radical rethink of the optimal approach to the category:

- 216,000 "super-heavy" drinkers accounted for 30.8 percent of market volume. These drinkers were worth over £800 per year.
- 2,136,000 combined "super-heavy/heavy" drinkers accounted for 77.9 percent of market volume with an annual worth of over £200 per year and offering the opportunity to generate £60 gross contribution.
- Light drinkers principally drank only on special occasions such as Christmas.
- The "super-heavy/heavy" user group purchased throughout the year buying, on average, a bottle every 11 weeks. They had

very distinctive characteristics in terms of geodemographics, demographics, lifestyles, attitudinal systems,
and media consumption. They had a highly targeted profile.

2. A segmentation brand model was built introducing the dimension of loyalty. This showed that the brand's volume dependency
was more biased toward the heavy user segment than the category
profile. This, however, totally reflected the brand's low level of penetration at the time relative to the brand leader (Index of 42). The
brand was being bought as part of a portfolio of brands. As such,
there was significant scope to build volume by both developing
brand loyalty and expanding brand penetration, as illustrated in
Table 4.3:

Table 4.3 Brand segmentation by usage and loyalty

User Segment: Category Usage	Brand Loyalty			
	Solus brand drinkers	"Most often" brand drinkers (60% loyal)	"Occasional" brand drinkers (20% loyal)	Total
Super Heavy/Heavy				
% of drinkers	3.2	12.3	16.6	32.1
% of volume	18.9	42.9	19.3	81.1
Medium				
% of drinkers	5.2	9.5	9.9	24.5
% of volume	4.9	5.4	1.9	12.1
Light				
% of drinkers	7.1	18.3	18.0	43.4
% of volume	2.2	3.5	1.1	6.8
Total				
% of drinkers	15.5	40.1	44.4	100
% of volume	26.0	51.8	22.3	100

A customer segmentation commercial business model was then constructed to show the actual and potential annual worth on the twin

dimensions of loyalty and usage. In terms of profit return per customer, the commercial priorities in ranking order, were:

- To convert current "super-heavy/heavy" occasional brand drinkers to become "most often" drinkers i.e., to become their preferred brand.
- To convert current "super-heavy/heavy" non-drinkers to become "occasional/most often" brand drinkers.
- To convert current "super-heavy/heavy most often" brand drinkers to become "solus" brand drinkers.
- To develop brand consumption among current "medium solus/most often" brand drinkers to become "heavy" users.

CRM Strategy

Deconstructing the brand into its different user groups quantified the degree to which the "heavy" user segment was strategically important to volume and profit and was identified as a strategically key target to attack over an extended time frame.

Hitherto, all customers were addressed the same with communication treating customers as a homogeneous mass. Marketing funds were focused on the pre-Christmas period with advertising and heavy in-store discounting. This was a very wasteful, inefficient way of spending finite marketing funds. It was not targeted marketing whilst being very expensive with the following negatives:

- All competing brands were doing exactly the same with, therefore, no clear brand standout.
- Advertising costs in the pre-Christmas period were at premium rates.
- The advertising decay factor meant that awareness levels were back down at pre-advertising rates within 3 months.
- In-store trade support costs were high as retailers played one brand off against another.
- Light buyers primarily purchased at Christmas either as a gift or as a reward for themselves, whereas the "heavy" user group bought throughout the year.

It was therefore decided to move toward a CRM model and marketing funds were diverted to engage a strategic relationship marketing program with the singular objective of building brand share among the "heavy" user group defined as 2+ bottles per year, either purchased for self-consumption or as a gift, by building penetration and weight of purchase. In so doing, to develop brand loyalty as a means of saving and protecting volume gains achieved.

The strategy to deliver the objectives is summarized as follows:

- To employ the principles of relationship marketing to positively influence consumer attitudes toward the brand as the means of changing behavior rather than simply bribery. Effectively using the power of advertising in communicating to the individual.
- Communication focused on the brand's values and imagery with target individuals feeling positively motivated toward the brand by the nature and content of the communication. Each communication was added value in nature and content with personal offers, information about new products and messages that uniquely personified the brand's physical and emotional attributes.
  Research showed that, irrespective of demographics, the common link knitting together the target group of users was their love of malt whisky. In essence, therefore, the communication took the distillery to the individual embracing him in the life, people, and happenings at the distillery.
- To use the customer database, once developed, to gather information on consumer attitudes, buying behavior, and consumer motivations behind the behavior.

The customer database progressively grew in size using highly targeted recruitment techniques including on-pack, affinity marketing partnerships, direct response advertising, and duty free promotions. In each case, consumers were invited to write in for a tasting notebook with questions on category and brand usage to complete as part of the application. The data capture covered:

- Name and address details including post code
- Gender
- Date of birth
- Where brand purchased
- Brand(s) of malt whisky personally drunk with list of brands and loyalty descriptors for each one: solus, most often, occasionally, never
- Frequency of buying malt whisky for drinking at home
- Number of bottles of malt whisky bought for personal use in the past year
- Number of bottles of malt whisky bought in last year to give as a gift
- Opt-in to receive future communication

This was used as the means of filtering out consumers who did not meet the usage requirements without them being aware of the action taken.

The creative design was universally applied across all communication pieces and was led by the brand's proposition and followed the above-the-line lead.

Members of the database received, on average, three items of communication per year via personalized post and, progressively, targeted tactical mailings addressing specific needs. Responses generated were exceedingly high to the various offers embracing "Introduce a Friend" (19 percent), free prize draws (40 percent), tailored coupons (13–40 percent), and exclusive product offers in which a purchase is made (5.5 percent). The latter, for example, achieved sales of over 500 bottles of a special edition malt at £175 per bottle. In parallel, members of the database were invited to hosted tasting sessions at venues round the country. Members paid to attend and they were always fully subscribed.

The "proof of the pudding is in the eating," in relation to how did the CRM program fare against payback criteria?

To measure this, a postal "tracker" questionnaire was used. The questionnaire incorporated the same questions featured in the recruitment questionnaire and was designed to measure changes in category/brand behavior relative to their behavior on recruitment as well as attitudes.

The annual tracker was mailed to the following format:

- No incentive was used to stimulate response
- The University of Lancaster, an authority on the application of statistics, laid down the sample composition to be representative of the database. The sample criteria was based on category usage, brand loyalty, and recency dimensions. The sample size was recommended at 8,000 assuming a 25 percent response rate
- In practice, the Tracker questionnaire was sent to a representative sample of 10,000 database residents with a response rate of 28 percent. It was a robust, representative sample that was statistically valid to a significance level of +/- 3 percent.

Results

1. The tracker surveys administered over an extended period of time showed the following:
   - Brand share moved from 38 percent on recruitment to 57 percent and was retained at that level.
   - Members of the database accounted for 52 percent of total brand sales and underpinned dynamic brand growth culminating in brand leadership.
   - The annual incremental net contribution generated by the CRM program, after allowing for CRM costs, contributed an increasingly majority share of overall brand profitability.
2. Breakeven was surpassed in Year 2 for each individual new recruit to the database.
3. An ROI of 215 percent was delivered over a 7 year time frame.

Targeted Marketing

There are three significant marketing benefits of adopting a CRM business model when applied through customer segmentation:

1. Provides a high grade targeting framework on three levels:
   A. It enables the selection of the optimal communication chan-
      nel(s) to reach and engage the target audience to acquire new
      customers. This results in both media efficiency and response
      effectiveness to be realized.
   B. The customer personas developed provide the means to craft
      communication messaging and content to maximize response
      when applied to both recruitment and retention activities.
   C. Customer retention and related loyalty can be targeted by
      segment.

A targeting framework is illustrated in Figure 4.4 based on a product/
service marketed to consumers.

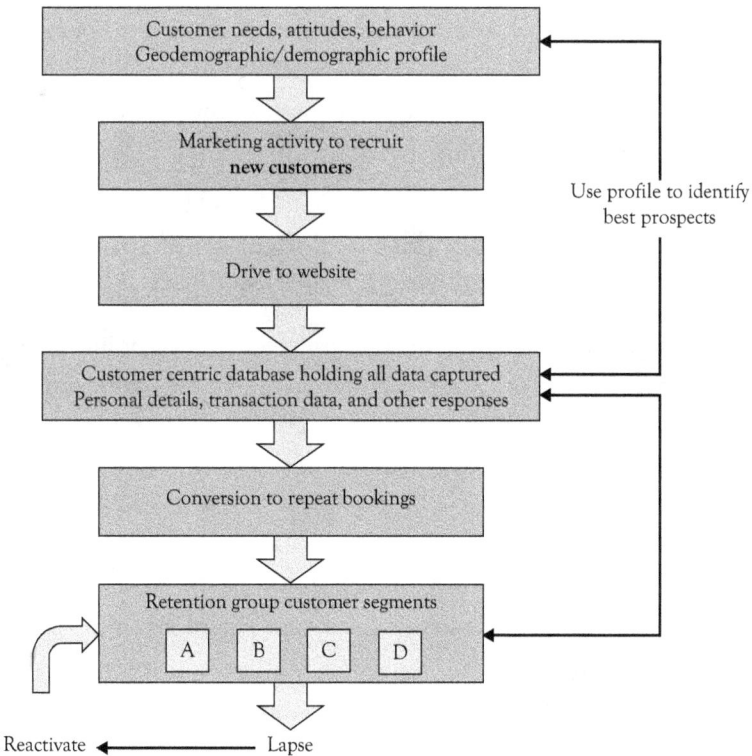

Figure 4.4 Targeted marketing framework

The important observations to note are:

- The customer centric database is the center of the data universe. In this context, profiling existing customers is the best way to define the target audience profile for new customer "best prospects" acquisition.
- Accurate profiling of the target audience for recruitment provides the platform to assess and select the optimal media channels to reach and convert them.
- The data captured and held on customer profiles and behavior yields the means to target those new recruits who have the greatest propensity to convert to repeat purchasing.
- Communication can be bespoke to the customer segments created using the RFV (Recency, Frequency, Value) model.
- Programs can be built into the customer database to recognize key customers who are about to lapse and to reactivate them immediately post lapsing if the first stage of communication did not deter them from lapsing.

Some Key Thoughts to Reflect on if You Are Considering/Reviewing CRM

CRM is a business strategy for the long haul requiring major investment in IT, processing systems, and organizational change but, on the upside, with the real potential of generating significant revenue and profit growth.

As such, the decision to engage a CRM strategy must be financially justified and robustly rooted in hard facts and quantified analysis.

A company should set out clear guidelines on the stringent and rigorous financial criteria for the CRM strategy to, in the first instance, be justified and thereafter measured against and judged accordingly. The component parts you should consider in developing and implementing a CRM strategy against this reference are:

- Have you built a Brand Equity Matrix?
- Have you developed a customer segmentation model?
- Have you set formal, quantified customer objectives?

- Have you fully and properly assessed and addressed the company's organizational capabilities and readiness to support the customer objectives in terms of technology, processes, the organizational structure, and working practices?
- Aligned the organization behind the goals?
- Developed the formal business model and strategy to deliver the objectives with a full ROI justification?
- Identified your brand proposition and differential benefits?
- Scoped out your relationship marketing strategy and associated platform to develop brand loyalty?
- Translated the strategy into a structured communications program by customer segment?
- Put in place a reporting structure that measures and reports on all key metrics in an actionable format in a timely fashion?
- Engaged a Targeted Marketing Framework to direct and control marketing expenditure with an emphasis on minimizing wastage through accurate targeting and maximizing response through relevant messaging at relevant times through the most appropriate media channels?

If you can tick all these boxes, you have the potential to create and execute a successful CRM strategy.

CHAPTER 5

The "C" in CRM

The Customer Rules the Roost

The customer rests at the epicenter of the CRM business model. The customer is KING.

A neat summary of the absolute importance of the customer was articulated by Mahatma Gandhi, father of the Indian nation (Dr. Babu 2016):

> "A customer is the most important visitor on our premises. He is not dependent on us; we are dependent on him. He is not an interruption in our work. He is the purpose of it. He is not an outsider in our business. He is part of it. We are not doing him a favour by serving him. He is doing us a favour by giving us the opportunity to do so."

The number 1 marketing commandment is: "KNOW YOUR CUSTOMER."

After all, in simple terms, if you don't really know them, how can you:

1. Realistically market products and services to meet their evolving needs and wants?
2. Target them effectively and efficiently in reaching them and eliciting a response by communicating motivating benefit-led messages with relevant content, copy style, and tone.

More significantly, the customer is a moving target. A company cannot remain aloof of change whilst the world in which many companies and brands operate in is a dynamic one. For example, for consumer products, change has and is occurring on so many dimensions such as those below:

A. Media channel fragmentation with media consumption now embracing broadcast and narrow cast options. The consumer choice is now endless in how they spend their leisure time consuming media:
- Program and content choices have been and are multiplying; supplied by streaming services, TV, and Film production companies. The transmission output is a one way, noninteractive communication. However, the recent phenomenon of social media platforms has changed the rules. Many social media users can and do create and communicate their own messages, which can include comments on brands based on their own experiences—good and bad—to their social media communities. Obviously, a brand neither controls nor is party to the conversation. Moreover, many of the messages are unstructured and make it difficult to extract and analyze to provide the insight to understand the rationale and motivations behind the views expressed.
- Where they take in their media consumption—on the move outside the home or at home/work in a static position.
- The application through which they watch/listen: TV, tablet, smartphone, laptop.
B. Demographic changes are factors in the composition of households stemming from, for example, sexuality, cultural, ethnic, and relationship status—working couples, single mums, and so on.
C. Seismic attitudinal shifts stimulated by media-led headline news on macro issues such as climate change impact on diet, transport, and in-home energy.
D. The online revolution directly influencing how consumers and businesses source information and buy products and services.

Thus, it is a case of crass stupidity for any company or brand to adapt an ostrich like stance and bury their head in the sand and blame other factors for a decline or closure of their business, when, in reality, it is because customers have changed and moved on and they have not been ahead of the curve in predicting and adapting to the change.

For example, in retailing:

- A Department Store proposition in the UK may have been highly relevant in 1800s/1900s, but not so today.
- Why did John Lewis not transform itself into an "Amazon"? It had the range and the supplier network to do so. John Lewis is the premier department store retailer in the GB market and is the ultimate reference for quality customer experience. Indeed, it was the bellweather for the retail sector trading performance.
- How did Sainsbury allow its market position to be usurped by Tesco?

I suggest because they were not looking externally on how the consumer (their customer) was changing with, in particular, a macro trend emerging on placing a premium on time and convenience as the joint working household became the norm and the work-life balance came more and more under the microscope.

Ignore the customer at your peril. Do not be complacent because you think you know your customer. Think outside the box and track how customer changes will potentially impact your business in identifying both opportunities and threats.

It may be a painful process and you do not like what you find, but there is nothing like a reality check and, unless you learn and act on the lessons, you may be too late. In the UK retail market, ask Mothercare, Woolworths, BHS, Debenhams, Laura Ashley, and Jessops, to name but a few, where we have witnessed their demise.

Obtaining the Information

You need to know your customers inside out. Fine but what does that mean?

Broadly, we need to know who they are, their buying behavior and the reasons behind their buying behavior. I outline a framework of what information is ideally required for each and the potential sources for obtaining it; using the consumer as our customer reference.

Profiles should be built for the "best customers" segment alongside the overall customer profile to identify any differences to help understand which characteristics make them the "best customers."

Who They Are?

Customer profiles cover the menu set out below with selections from the list ultimately made based on those deemed to influence demand and targeting methodology:

A. Standard demographics with a comprehensive pen portrait: Age, sex, marital status, social class, location, children by age group, ethnic background, sexuality, religion, home status (type, value, ownership), education/professional qualifications, household income.

B. Geodemographic profile.

C. Lifestyle interests: hobbies, sport participation and viewing, holidays, club membership, eating out (visit pubs and/or restaurants), media consumption by channel type including TV subscription services, support charities by type.

D. Status: Wealth (investments by type, savings, property ownership), other financial product usage (credit cards, insurances by type), employment position, consumer durable ownership, digital equipment ownership/usage (smartphone, digital cameras, tablets, laptops, digital satellite TV, smartwatch, fitness band, etc.), car ownership (number and models).

E. Online usage via any device—mobile, laptop/PC and tablet/iPad—by frequency of use:

- Online activity: Such as gambling/betting, managing personal finances, online auctions, online shopping, sourcing information on products/services, watching films/TV, playing games, streaming/watching live events, sending pictures, receiving/redeeming coupons/vouchers, booking tickets, paying for things on mobile phone, online dating, accessing news, school/university work.

- Research online: For example, financial products/services, government services/departments, household utilities, travel, holidays, eating out, days out, hotels, airline time-

tables/costs/availability, gardening products, music, books/
videos/DVD's, clothes/accessories, groceries/drinks, cost
comparison sites, cars, home improvements

- Buy online: Such as financial products/services, travel/
  airline tickets, holidays, hotel reservations, restaurant reservations, groceries and drink, clothes/accessories, gardening
  products, live events (music, sports, exhibitions, etc.), days
  out, utilities.

F. Use of social media: number of hours per week, channel used
(Facebook, Twitter, LinkedIn, Instagram, etc.), how used (contact
universe by profile and scale, communication content, motivations
and needs satisfied at emotional and functional levels).

G. General attitude sets: attitudes toward health, the environment,
business, appearance, and so on.

The following sources should be explored to obtain the information
required:

1. The first port of call should be the customer database to check what
   data is currently held against the above template. In so doing, isolate
   the "best customer" segments to receive particular attention because
   their profile will form the bullseye to target new acquisition customers.

   One of the most important data capture variables is the postcode because this is the link to other external data sets that can be
   used for profiling.

2. Geodemographic systems using the postcode to profile the customer database against the national adult universe (e.g., GB). This
   performs two roles:

   a. Firstly, the degree of bias with customers potentially concen-
      trated into a small number of geodemographic types which, if
      so, will form the core descriptors and act as the reference for
      developing pen portraits. Each type has a profile attached, put
      together by the geodemographic company.

   b. Secondly, the geodemographic universe can be overlaid with
      external data sets to enrich the profile. For example, in the UK,
      the Target Group Index (TGI) data bank can provide much of

the data parameters identified above linked to each geodemographic type.

3. Conduct an online market research survey among the customer database residents.
4. Conduct an online market research survey using an external panel with the sample composition being representative of the customer universe; using the customer database profile as the reference, and the size and structure of the sample supporting statistically valid results.
5. Use external databanks to profile the customer database.

Their Buying Behavior

There are a number of measures of buying behavior to explore with the final specification dependent on your type of business and the sector in which it operates. Metrics cover the following variables:

- How often do they buy?
- How long have they been a customer?
- When did they last buy?
- How much did they buy?
- How much do they buy at one time?
- When do they buy?
- Is there a pattern to their buying; for example, seasonal?
- What do they buy?
- How much do they spend?

The potential sources of information to assess are:

Primarily, the current customer database in applying the customer segmentation model developed. From this, you can clearly see where each customer sits and their relative importance to financial contribution. This obviously is restricted to an absolute measure of current customers, in isolation of their overall sector behavior.

Secondly, to assess the brand's relative position within its sector. This can be evaluated in one of the three ways mentioned below:

1. Recourse to an external panel where the panel records and measures buying behavior in your relevant sector. Panels are run, for example, in

the UK, by TGI, Kantar, and Nielsen. These are ongoing panels with varying frequencies and different methodologies of collecting data.

2. Conducting an online market research survey across the customer database.

3. Conducting an online market research survey using an external panel with the size and composition of the sample being statistically representative and valid.

Reasons Behind Their Buying Behavior

We need to understand why customers behave the way they do, with differences identified between each loyalty group: solus, most often, occasional, and never brand buyers.

To gain a deep understanding of customers' needs and wants, their beliefs and motivations of relevance to their buying behavior in the sector and brands within it as well as alternatives to the sector; for example, buying online as an alternative to high street retailers.

This rests at the heart of marketing, but is a very difficult area to probe and gauge sensitivities because humans have a complex make-up and do not always behave and think in a rational way.

For example, in the stampede to online buying. Presumably there has always been a need for convenient shopping but what has caused the acceleration to this channel of shopping? One or a combination of all of the following factors have contributed to this radical change in consumer behavior:

- Improved security; in perception and/or in reality of online payment systems
- Return policies of suppliers
- Wider choice of online shopping options
- Trusted retailer brands offering an online option
- Increase in number of homes with working couples placing increased emphasis on convenience
- Consumers placing more emphasis on the quality of life and how to spend quality time, thereby downgrading time spent on functional, day-to-day living
- Improved navigation of shopping websites
- Online product innovation

- Word of mouth spreading confidence from recommendations of friends/family/colleagues based on their personal online shopping experiences
- Media exposure and increasing awareness to the point where this shopping channel becomes the norm

Consumers' expectations and aspirations are evolving, which means "wants" rise in the hierarchy of understanding and explaining consumers' behavior. Exploring the more emotional territory of what makes consumers tick is a research challenge. Getting under the skin of what really matters to consumers requires a rigorous, multipronged approach that accepts people do not necessarily understand their own motivations.

As Rory Sutherland of Ogilvy once said, "We don't know why we do the things we do. Moreover, the reasons we do attach to our behaviour are often a post-rationalisation and therefore really an explanation as much designed to make us look good and sensible as it is a truthful response to the question." (Charlotte Rogers, Missing the Point: Why brands are failing to get the most from customer insight, *Marketing Week* August 12, 2019). I feel sure this applies to the move to online shopping in the reference above. For example, have consumers stopped to think what happens when there are no high street retailers to pop in and look at merchandise and seek professional advice as in, for example, John Lewis in the UK on digital consumer equipment.

Thus, dependent on the complexity of the issues to interrogate, it is imperative to work with your market research professionals to explore how best to seek and obtain the answers to the questions you have. There are a range of techniques but the most important challenge is to define the questions and attitude scales to use as the means of eliciting the response. They need to be sensitive to the nuances of the responses and be able to calibrate the relative importance of these.

In terms of the research universe, the first port of call is the customer base in interacting with customers to understand their expectations and their relationships with brands. The questionnaire and research approach can be finetuned via this route before extending to a wider audience.

(Steve Hemsley, How customer experience is building brands and business, *Marketing Week* June 19, 2019), (Trevor Parsons, True customer-centricity requires proper investment, *Marketing Week* August 12, 2019), (Rather 2016), (Salim 2018).

Brand Proposition

Having done the hard graft, don't rest on your laurels. You now have a clear understanding of what your current and potential customer "needs and wants" are and what "turns them on and off."

The final cross on the graph is to define how you are going to meet your customers' "needs and wants" and clearly position your brand to address and communicate them. This is the territory of defining brand benefits; ideally, a unique proposition with differential benefits to separate your brand from the competition. This is a significant marketing challenge to distill all the research findings and insights, and translate into a clear benefit-led brand proposition. The output should be a formal written brand positioning statement signed off by the Board and communicated across the business and external agencies as the **BRAND BIBLE**. This is the reference that drives all external communication to customers and, as such, is the ongoing check for ensuring all such communication is "on brand."

Different companies employ different processes to arrive at their Brand Positioning Statement and different templates to express it. One suggested approach is tabled below using a fictitious UK restaurant chain (Café Fleur) as the brand reference with the aim of illustrating the "headings" to guide the process.

Café Fleur is a French brasserie style casual dining restaurant with boutique style hotel accommodation attached. In concept, it is similar to the French "Logis" where the focus is on the restaurant with the hotel accommodation as the "add-on"; albeit done to a chic, high quality, design-led, and stylish specification. Each location has its own unique character; once again reflecting the French "Logis" where each one is independently owned and family run with a focus on their passion for superb food and customer service. The group currently consists of 10 locations that are carefully located in middle class towns with good access to trunk road routes.

Using this as our guide, the Brand Positioning Statement is set out in Table 5.1.

Table 5.1 Brand positioning statement

BRAND POSITIONING STATEMENT CAFÉ FLEUR

A. TARGET AUDIENCE

A.1. Demographics
Female adults aged 45+
Above average household income: £50K+
No children at home

A.2. Geodemographics
Based on CACI's Acorn Geodemographic system
a) Primary: Affluent Achievers
- Wealthy, high status rural, semirural, and suburban areas of the country
- Middle aged or older people with many empty nesters and wealthy retired
- Well-off families with older children at University or left home
- Large detached houses
- Well educated and employed in managerial and professional occupations
- Can afford to spend freely and frequently with savings and investments
- Usually confident with new technology
- Healthy, wealthy, and confident consumers
b) Secondary: Comfortable Communities
- Middle of the road Britain
- Covers all life stages. Mixed areas—some contain stable families, empty nesters, comfortably off pensioners living in retirement areas around the coast, and sometimes younger couples starting out their lives together
- Generally owner occupiers living in semi-detached or detached houses of average or marginally above average value in the region
- Overall household income marginally above average
- Employment in a mix of professional, managerial, clerical, and skilled occupants
- Educational qualifications in line with the national average
- Most are comfortably off
- They may not be overtly wealthy but they have few major financial worries

A.3. Lifestyle/Attitudes
Discriminating and discerning people with confidence in their decision making.
Time rich with the income to enjoy life in which socializing is an integral part.
Interest in food and eating out are central themes in their lifestyle. Eating out is in their DNA with a high frequency of dining out with either their partner or adult friends. In so doing, they have a preference for local restaurants and pubs over national chains.

B. BRAND PROPOSITION

Café Fleur: Enjoy good food and good company in the adult, relaxed ambience of your local French brasserie where you can experience the French passion for food, people, conversation and, above all, the panache in everything we do.

Table 5.1 (Continued)

C. SUPPORT FOR THE PROPOSITION

1. Quantified Research among the customer universe robustly confirmed that Café Fleur possesses major differential strengths. It's appeal directly relates to the core brand proposition, which was reflected and reinforced by the Net Promoter Scores (see Chapter 11) it achieved in research on ratings for Café Fleur:

   - The quality of the food and drink offering   = +65%
   - The recipes of dishes on the menu   = +57%
   - Friendly service   = +53%
   - The environment/atmosphere   = +49%

   These are really remarkable scores and provide the platform on which to build a benefit-led consumer proposition that differentiates Café Fleur from other restaurants; particularly, premium casual dining groups.
   More importantly, it resonates and connects with its target audience, which, in marketing terms, is "worth its weight in gold."

2. The primary competition to Café Fleur at local level are independent restaurants and pubs. Café Fleur sits comfortably within this trading environment with an extraordinary level of front of mind awareness and visit frequency and, importantly, is not perceived to be pigeon holed in the premium casual dining category.

3. Durable, true brand loyalty is based on customer satisfaction. Satisfaction derived from the brand experience in which the brand continuously meets or exceeds customer expectations. This is directly linked to the functional and/or emotional benefits the brand delivers which are the core brand attributes.
   In this respect, Café Fleur demonstrably delivers both functional and emotional benefits in meeting customers' needs and wants.

4. Café Fleur understands and identifies with the world of its customers in which good food and wine shared with good company are an important part. Café Fleur wants to share its passion for food and wine and the people who make the dining out experience an enjoyable one with them. This is an emotional bridge in connecting the brand with its customers.

5. Café Fleur restaurants are unique properties peculiar to their location. They do not follow a common property design like Café Rouge or Cote (these are Casual Dining chains in GB) and, as such, can more readily be accepted as part of the local trading environment in which they have a unique brand positioning. Importantly, the stylish, boutique accommodation adds an extra dimension to divert away from direct comparisons.

6. The marketing communications of premium casual dining groups is not benefit-led with a creative proposition that is uniformly communicated across all customer touch points. They are not providing a benefit-led reason(s) why anyone should visit their restaurants. Their communication is features-led with an emphasis on promotions.

(Continued)

Table 5.1 (Continued)

D. CUSTOMER BELIEFS

External communication should engender the following set of beliefs for the brand:
- There is no better place to enjoy a really relaxing and enjoyable dining experience.
- When I choose Café Fleur, I know I am going to be treated as I would like to be treated.
- Café Fleur understands and identifies with me as a customer in everything they do.
- When I leave Café Fleur, I have a somewhat smug smile on my face because of the wonderful food and wine I have dined on.
- It's oh so nice to be able to relax in an adult orientated dining environment.
- I want to give a hug to all the kitchen staff for serving me such a tasty and interesting menu.
- Wow, how do they maintain such high quality standards?

E. BRAND PERSONALITY

Warm, personable, sociable, witty, outgoing without being extrovert, charming, enthusiastic, and passionate about their work

---

Some Key Thoughts to Reflect on if You Are Considering/Reviewing CRM

CRM Starts and Ends With the Customer

You are not in the CRM race unless you know your customers inside out. The company's marketing team must "live and breathe" the customer and ensure the Board of Directors do the same!

Easily said than done because, as human beings, customers often behave in an irrational, emotional way and, most significantly, their attitude set is constantly shifting; sometimes at the most incredible speed as witnessed by the 2020 pandemic (Covid-19).

The two sacrosanct rules to adopt are:

- Know your customers.
- Do not treat them as a homogeneous mass. Recognize that individual customers' personalities can vary from one to the other and can often be grouped together as clusters with common characteristics according to their behavior, profile, interests, and attitude set or a combination of all.

To this end, you must:

- Know who they are.
- Know their buying behavior.
- Know the reasons behind their buying behavior.
- Know their general attitudes toward shopping (for consumers), the environment, and other factors that could have an impact on buying your products/services.
- Put in place a sophisticated, robust, and well-constructed ongoing market research methodology to keep your "finger on the pulse" of customer attitude and behavior shifts in general and specific to your market sector(s).

Finally, and most importantly, translate your insights and understanding into formalizing your brand proposition. In simple terms, why should customers buy your brand in preference to other brands? Place your brand proposition at the center of your Brand Positioning Statement, which directs and controls all external customer communication. All creativity in terms of style, tone, and content is driven by the Brand Positioning Statement. It is the brand's creative bible.

If you are unable to define a relevant brand proposition that imparts clear and differential benefits to your target audience, I would surmise you are either already in trouble or are heading for trouble!

CHAPTER 6

The "R" in CRM²

CRM is commercially driven. Resting at the heart of CRM is maximizing profit through customer development with a focus on "best customers"—those that contribute most to revenue and profit. To identify "best prospect" customers, reach and convert them and develop them into ongoing loyalty. BUT, what is loyalty and how do we nurture and own it? Implicit in the definition of brand loyalty is the existence of a relational bridge existing between the brand and the customer. A commitment that underpins an emotional bond manifesting itself in a public declaration of "It's my brand of choice" by the customer. This is the "R" in CRM: the relationship between the company (brand) and its customers.

Let's start by taking a helicopter view on loyalty in relation to some "super brand" icons. Customer loyalty is the most precious commodity in the currency of brands: carefully built, vigorously defended, and yet easily eroded by the complacent.

However, some brands that have invested year after year in delivering excellent consumer value, consistent quality, and reliable service still do not generate high loyalty.

So, what is the added ingredient in a "Superbrand" that brings consumers back time after time again? I judge it is a unique combination of trust, affection, and REAL CONSUMER BENEFITS that are repeatedly delivered over time, which generates lasting consumer loyalty.

Look at the record of "Superbrands" (e.g., in the UK: Tesco, Land Rover, Burberry, Cadbury, BMW, Gillette, Fairy, Coca-Cola, Apple, Lego, Sky, Dulux, Kit-Kat, Audi, and Dyson). Look at their consistent and relentless pursuit of consumer satisfaction, constantly listening, constantly learning, constantly improving, seeking to innovate and, above all, never allowing their offering to stagnate.

So, why do "Superbrands" command higher loyalty? Simply put, because they provide us with **real benefits** and consistent superior, genuine satisfaction. That's why we love them.

And that's why we need to explore and understand customer loyalty. It is the marketing Holy Grail to optimize ongoing, sustainable profit.

We explore this vital topic under the following headings:

1. Why is loyalty important?
2. What is loyalty?
3. Who to build a loyalty relationship with?
4. How to build a relationship—Relationship Marketing?
5. What steps to take?
6. What loyalty programs to offer?

Why Is Loyalty Important?

1. Media and audience fragmentation, coupled with the dynamic of online buying, has led to a fundamental shift in the business model. From a "Mass Marketing" approach, in which the product was the primary focus, to a "Micro Marketing" approach, where the pivotal focus is the customer. This is illustrated below in Figure 6.1 for a consumer product or service:

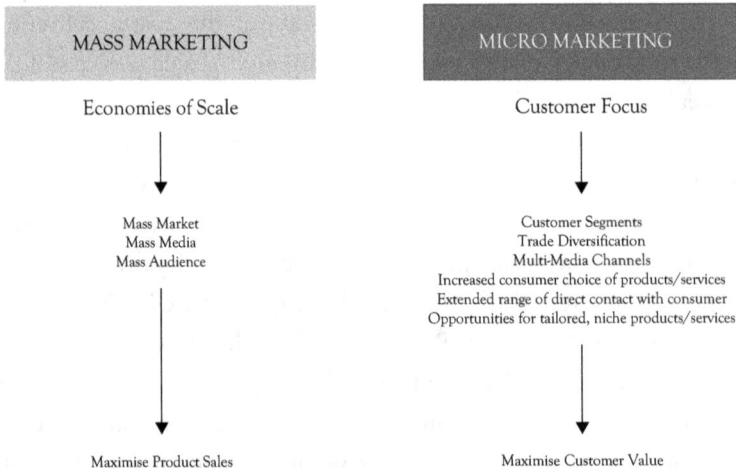

MASS MARKETING	MICRO MARKETING
Economies of Scale	Customer Focus
↓	↓
Mass Market Mass Media Mass Audience	Customer Segments Trade Diversification Multi-Media Channels Increased consumer choice of products/services Extended range of direct contact with consumer Opportunities for tailored, niche products/services
↓	↓
Maximise Product Sales	Maximise Customer Value

Figure 6.1 Changing market place

Many, if not most, consumer markets have become more intensely competitive whilst, in parallel, more mature. More companies chasing the same consumer where power has irreversibly shifted to the consumer; who is savvy enough to know how to leverage such power in their brand selections. In this context, the importance of loyalty escalates in the pursuit of profitability. It becomes progressively expensive to pursue and win new customers whilst brands are surrounded by a load of "brand sharks" waiting to pounce and take a brand's customers away from them. It is an imperative for a brand to become a "Fort Knox and pull up the drawbridge," repel all brand assailants and keep their precious, "best loyal" customers. Customer retention and development of loyalty is the top commercial priority for all brands.

It is not surprising that brand leaders in product categories are those that enjoy the highest level of brand loyalty among their customer base.

The consumer map will become ever more complex and the demands on companies to respond accordingly will correspondingly escalate. The impact of technology on the way we think and behave, and on our attitudes will be unprecedented. The scale of upheaval and disruption with AI (Artificial Intelligence), genetic engineering, climate change, driverless cars, and so on is already reshaping society and the political landscape. The consumer universe is likely to fragment to even smaller segments with differences in outlook, lifestyle, diet, attitudes, and the work/leisure balance. Companies that have not already recognized and embraced a customer centric business model will find it ever more difficult to commercially survive in such a progressive world. Identifying "best customers" and adapting products and services to meet their evolving needs and wants and, in so doing, cement their loyalty will be of paramount financial importance.

2. It is a well-known, established commercial fact that a small proportion of a brand's consumers account for a larger proportion of its revenue—the "80:20" rule (The Pareto Principle); although, in practice, more likely to be 70:30 or even 60:40. These customers tend to

be the biggest spenders and the most loyal as demonstrated in their repeat purchasing behavior. This is conceptually illustrated below in Figures 6.2 and 6.3:

Hence, in pure commercial terms, it is a "no brainer" not to initially focus on the "best customers" and put in place a clear and cohesive strategy to address their needs and wants before chasing other goals. Financially, it is an absolute **MUST** to nurture and retain this group and ring fence them from competition.

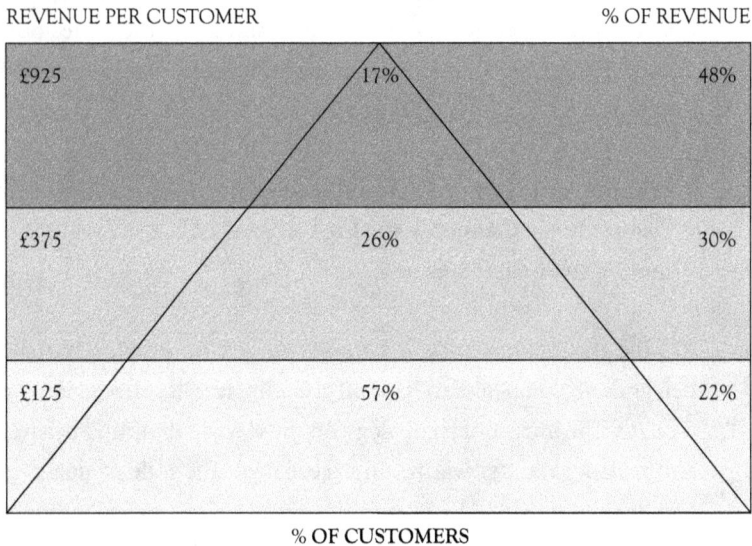

REVENUE PER CUSTOMER   % OF REVENUE

£925	17%	48%
£375	26%	30%
£125	57%	22%

% OF CUSTOMERS

Based on an alcoholic drink brand

Figure 6.2 Source of revenue based on an alcoholic drink brand

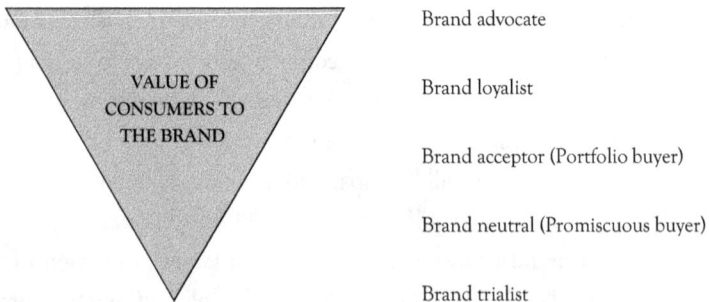

VALUE OF
CONSUMERS TO
THE BRAND

Brand advocate

Brand loyalist

Brand acceptor (Portfolio buyer)

Brand neutral (Promiscuous buyer)

Brand trialist

Figure 6.3 Consumer value to a brand

3. Loyalty is a strategic issue. The potential financial prize is enormous by retaining and developing a customer's lifetime value (CLV). For example, for multiple supermarkets in GB. If they meet customers' needs at all stages through their lifetime, we are talking about a customer's lifetime value of circa £95,000—effectively treating the customer as an individual profit center. When a company consistently delivers superior value, stemming from a combination of complete product satisfaction and value added customer experience, it results in rising customer loyalty. In turn, market share and revenues go up and the cost of acquiring and servicing customers goes down. The economic benefits of customer loyalty often explains why one competitor is more profitable than another.

   CLV (see Chapter 11) is an integral part of the CRM vocabulary with the concept amplified by Pfeifer and Bang: "Customer long term value (CLV) of a customer is the present value of the future cash flows attributable to the customer relationship over the lifetime of that relationship." (Pfeifer and Bang 2005)

4. There is a growing overall level of consumer fatigue in many product/service categories. Few brands really stand clear in terms of differential benefits, especially functional ones. Brands move to a common point where, in terms of physical characteristics and functional performance, they are near identical. The effect is seen in the gradual erosion of the brand's franchise and in greater consumer promiscuity.

   In such circumstances, the brand's business model comes under pressure because of the lack of protection in defending against either changing market conditions or competitive attack; particularly to combat any external factors impacting either demand or margins, or both. For example, cost pressures squeeze margins, which cannot be alleviated through the pricing mechanism because of the lack of a core loyal customer segment and the lack of a clear product proposition giving real benefits of why consumers should choose one brand in preference to another. The 2020 casual dining restaurant sector in GB is a classic example of this phenomenon in action. Indeed, the restaurants line up in the same location to emphasize their commonalities. Moreover, their prevailing solution to the problem is through the promotion route with couponing and discounting with, in the main, all customers treated the same and the communication take out by the recipient being a feeling of being "sold to." This is trying to "buy" short term business because *you cannot buy loyalty!*

In a commoditized market, the quality and depth of a customer's relationship with a brand must be the ultimate differentiator on which the loyalty bond with the customer is founded. This is explored below in the section on Relationship Marketing.

What Is Loyalty?*[3]

Defining loyalty is not a simplistic case of measuring behavior. We also need to question the reasons behind the behavior to understand how secure and sustainable the loyalty status actually is? And that is where we can hit the buffers because not all behavior is rational!

Customer loyalty is a fusion of superior product/service satisfaction and the emotional attachment to the brand stemming from their customer experiences and their connection with the brand's value system and positioning. The latter is reflected in its imagery, its pricing, and its quality. Above all, the benefits (functional and/or emotional) the brand offers and delivers and the extent to which they are unique. From this, it is evident that a brand **must:**

- **Monitor and understand customer needs and wants as they evolve over time.**
- **Continuously respond to them through product development and enhancement with a serious commitment to do so ingrained in the company's ethos.**
- **Continuously refresh and refine the brand offering and communication to stay connected and relevant to reflect changing attitudes, demographics, and lifestyles.**
- **Ensure the customer receives a consistent added value experience across all touch points with the brand in tune with the brand's positioning.**

We can see that durable, true customer loyalty is based on a combination of factors; principally overt positive attitudes toward the brand and supreme product/service delivery. The result is one of complete customer trust in and commitment to the brand, translating into the ultimate loyalty state of being a brand advocate in which the customer rejoices in his or her choice and happily recommends it to friends, family, and colleagues. At its core is customer satisfaction. Satisfaction derived from the brand experience at every touch point with the brand in which the brand continuously meets or exceeds expectations: time after time.

There are some critical guidelines to take on board when interrogating and expanding our understanding of customer loyalty, which are explored below:

1. The most important guide of all at the epicenter of building loyalty—the product or service continues to deliver ongoing real benefits that directly meet evolving customer needs and wants. In the context of the latter, we are often talking about emotional benefits rather than functional benefits and such benefits could have a different focus by customer segment.

   For example, in the dishwasher tablet market, the umbrella proposition is all about the functional benefit of impeccable clean dishes with a perfect shine every time communicated through broadscale media.

   However, there is a very important segment of users of Mums with babies and young children who are big volume users. Here, the most relevant benefit is a more emotional one of time—the most precious gift you can give your baby—by spending time with your baby and not your dishes! "Taking time to help your baby become the best they can be." More importantly, Mums can do so knowing their dishwasher and tablet are looking after their dishes in the most hygienic way; washing dishes at up to 70 degrees C, killing all germs. It also allows Mums to kiss goodbye to germs spread by endless dishcloths and tea towels. A win-win situation. The communication channel here is ideally "one-to-one marketing" through personalized direct mail to be able to effectively communicate an emotional message in a highly targeted manner.

This means a fundamental, **total** company commitment to tracking customer needs/wants and adjusting the physical characteristics of the product/service and its brand proposition and positioning accordingly. A continuous market research program that enables the company to track changing attitudes and how they translate into purchasing requirements. Indeed, to set your stall out to be ahead of the curve in predicting changes (e.g., Tesco's move to out-of-town stores) rather than responding to changes (e.g., Marks & Spencer's late entry to online grocery shopping via Ocado). Both are UK market related.

2. Loyalty is not simply a behavioral state. Loyalty measurement is not one-dimensional because it does not take into account the reasons for their purchase behavior status.

Many customers can be judged to be loyal according to their purchase measurement behavior and how they respond to research questionnaires on dimensions of customer satisfaction but such interpretation can be misleading.

Firstly, just because purchase measurements indicate loyalty, does not mean the customer is attitudinally loyal. Two examples here:

- Workers commuting into London hate the service but keep buying the season ticket because, logistically, they believe they have no practical choice or the alternatives carry even more negatives; for example, traveling by car. Conducting attitudinal research will elicit the true feelings behind the purchase and, presented with competitive choice, many customers would be off like a shot. In essence, they consider themselves "trapped" because they do not see a realistic choice. They often experience very poor service but have to accept it. But they will be vocal in their displeasure and will take every opportunity to complain and seek the service they expect. Sharing their experiences by "word of mouth" can deter new customers being acquired. As such, it remains in the commercial interest of the brand owner to proactively improve the service to deliver sustainable long-term profits and, in the case of the railways, provide a defensible case to protect their franchise.

- Airline travelers using loyalty programs may be recorded
  as frequent, loyal fliers. However, attitudinal research may
  establish that they are highly critical of the service and the
  only reason they travel is to earn the rewards. (Note: there
  is a difference in loyalty programs rewarding loyalty rather
  than trying to "buy" loyalty through price discounting.)
  The obvious route is to deliver superior customer service
  alongside the rewards as exemplified by Tesco.

Beware that behavior patterns can hide a false loyalty position with a variety of factors generating such a perspective:

- Lack of competition. For example, commuter railways
- Government regulations limiting competition
- High switching costs to move from one supplier to another
- Proprietary technology limiting alternatives
- Strong loyalty promotion programs

Secondly, customer satisfaction measurement. How many markets have we seen where, in B2C, over 80 percent report being satisfied but only 40 percent repurchase or, in B2B, 65 percent of defectors had previously declared they were satisfied or very satisfied. There are two factors at work here that need to be accounted for:

- The scale used to measure satisfaction can be anything
  from a 5 point scale (very dissatisfied to very satisfied)
  to a 10 point scale to expand the sensitivity. In either
  case, only the extreme score should be interpreted as a
  measure of satisfaction to take account, for example, of
  the UK consumers' penchant for not wanting to upset
  people. For a 5 point scale, just use the "very satisfied"
  score and avoid the temptation to combine "satisfied"
  and "very satisfied" as a measure of satisfaction. On a
  10 point scale, use the NPS approach (see Chapter 11)
  and combine the scores for 9 and 10. These give a truer
  indication of the real satisfaction status.
- Run a series of attitude questions alongside the satisfaction question and cross analyze to correlate the degree of
  attitudinal loyalty with the declared satisfaction score.

In summary, there is a profound difference between attitudinal loyalty and behavioral loyalty. A customer is behaviorally loyal if they continue buying a brand (or from a company), while an attitudinally loyal customer is one who **prefers** to buy a particular brand (or from a specific company). If the customer's loyal behavior is not driven by the customer's own positive attitude about their purchase, the relationship will be highly vulnerable to competition. For example, that's one of the potential drawbacks of using price discounts to acquire new customers. These are the ones who are more sensitive to pricing issues than they are to other factors such as quality and they will be the first to defect to competitors offering their own discounts.

As stated above, assessing customers' attitudinal loyalty requires ongoing survey work whilst behavioral loyalty can be objectively observed.

This is illustrated in papers by Don Peppers (Customer Loyalty: Behaviour or Attitude, *Marketing Week* May 7, 2019), Malthouse and Mulhern (2007), and Peter and Olson (2004).

This is the crux of loyalty. True brand loyalty occurs when the product or service exceeds expectations and delivers an unprecedented experience. Once a brand's promise is delivered, it is important to stoke the fires to prompt both behavioral and attitudinal loyalty thereby increasing purchase frequency and AOV (Average Order Value). Loyalty marketing features such as personalization and targeted marketing campaigns provide relevant content to enhance the customer experience. Like all successful relationships, the more relevant, fresh, and richer the content, the better the chance to sustain the relationship (see following section on Relationship Marketing).

3. There are degrees of loyalty as measured by their behavior. A suggested hierarchy is:
   • ACTIVE LOYALS: Attitudinal loyal customers. Hard-core loyal customers who buy a specific brand all the time as their preferred brand. They are solus buyers who allocate 100 percent of their spend in the category on the specific brand. These are brand advocates.

- PASSIVE LOYALS: Behavioral loyal customers. Buy a specific brand all the time but purchase is more of inertia and indifference driven. They are solus buyers who allocate 100 percent of their spend in the category on the specific brand.

- SPLIT LOYALS: Semi-loyal customers who buy 2–3 brands but allocate the majority of spend in the category to the specific brand. They can be classified as "Most Often" brand buyers with, as a guideline, the brand accounting for about 60 percent of the customer's category spend.

- SHIFTING LOYALS: Customers who move from one brand to another. They are portfolio buyers. They can be classified as "occasional brand buyers" with, as a guideline, the brand accounting for about 20 percent of the customer's category spend. They find the brands in their portfolio to be acceptable in meeting their purchasing criteria. They are brand discriminators and make a positive selection on a range of criteria and not price alone. For example, the confectionery category.

- SWITCHERS: Promiscuous buyers who exhibit absolutely no loyalty. They respond to low prices, buy on impulse, react to fashion trends or make change for the sake of making a change. The majority buy on price alone. They chase the "promotion dragon" and, in marketing parlance, are often referred to as "promotion junkies." They are expensive to recruit but quick to leave. Certainly, they do not stay long enough for the relationship to turn into profit. Brands gain little in marketing to this group even though many continue to do so; simply because they cannot tell them apart from the others!

Obviously, the ranking and customer count for each classification will vary according to the size of the category and the brand choice available to the buyer.

The marketing thrust will be one of focusing on moving as many target "best prospects" into the "Active Loyals" classification and minimizing investment in the "Switchers" classification.

The significance of loyalty as a brand and commercial factor is highlighted in the following quotes:

- "Long-term customers buy more, bring in new customers, take less of the service provider's time and are less sensitive to price." (Reichheld 1996)
- "Brand loyalty is more than just repeat buying behaviour; it also includes a preference for a particular brand and a positive emotional response to the brand." (Arnold, Price, and Zinkhan 2003)
- "Loyalty status is an important segmentation basis and allows for distinction between consumers who always buy the same brand (hard-core loyals) and those that are loyal to 2 or more brands (split loyals)." (Kotler and Keller 2005)
- "Managing successful customer relationships begins with identifying and acquiring the right customers. Therefore, companies must strive to discover who are their best customers and gain their loyalty whilst simultaneously allocating fewer resources to manage relationships with unprofitable customers." (Kimiloglu and Zarali 2009)

4. "Word of mouth" recommendation remains the strongest introduction to a brand. And the arrival and widespread use of social media has expanded its role with communities built from the small to the enormous acting as the medium for "chat." This is both a highly prized and sensitive medium because an influential message, good or bad, impacting on a brand's image can be carried to a cast of thousands at the click of a button. More importantly, the brand owner has no control over the original message which, if derogatory, could be really harmful and yet be emotionally led and not based on factual information.

In this context, it must be recognized that "word of mouth" can be negative as well as positive with the former conveying messages of "poor brand experiences." There are two policies for a company to adopt to fully acknowledge the power of the medium and the role of "word of mouth":

- No company is perfect and mistakes can be made resulting in a customer having a bad experience and, in the main, customers understand this. The question is how a company responds to such situations?

It is imperative that a company has "best practice" customer service in place to act positively and treat customers exceptionally well and with respect when things go wrong. A company should aim to turn this situation to its best advantage by overtly being seen to make amends. If so, a customer's belief in the company is made even more enduring because customers are essentially reasonable. They will applaud a professional service where they see themselves as the focus of attention, with their rights recognized, and the ability to express themselves allowed for.

> The biggest risk is those who desert with a "chip on their shoulder" and, as a result of their bad experience, will feel unloved and poorly done by. To them, no one listened, no one responded and no one sorted out their problem. They will potentially vent their full frustration.

This reinforces the need for tackling the issue head on wherever it occurs—in a restaurant, at a hotel reception, online, telephone customer service, and so on. The policy for addressing the customer should be uniformly applied across all customer interfaces with customer service and customer care of an exceptional standard. More importantly, make the opportunity to complain accessible—not hanging on a telephone line for an hour (British Airways take note) or the brand hiding behind their online presence with the only contact route being via e-mail. At the bottom line, prevention is the only real solution.

Remember, a hard-done customer (in the eyes of the customer) is capable of spreading vitriol to a really wide audience but is equally capable of spreading goodwill if treated like "royalty." The case study below clearly illustrates the extreme of "Bad Practice" to punch home the importance of professional customer management.

- In many product/service categories, the modern-day customer has several touch points with the company. For example, the website, e-mail communication to and from the customer database, enquiries via the website, electronic ordering and delivery tracking, telephone booking and customer services, and so on. In each case, the customer experience should be a uniform one and to the policy quality standards set by the company; ideally a "gold standard" with the customer treated as the "special one." This needs to be translated into measurable criteria. For example, call on a customer contact line being answered within "X" minutes with ideally a message telling the customer where they are in the queue. In contrast, how many of us have made a call to a company customer contact number and sat on the telephone for 15 minutes or more with a repeated message telling us how important we are!

The importance of word-of-mouth is underscored in the following quotes:

- "Positive word-of-moth relates to customer value because a customer who influences the purchases of other customers is of greater value to a firm." (Dick and Bask 1994)
- Jeff Bezos of Amazon made two pertinent observations: "If you build a great experience, customers tell each other about that. Word-of-mouth is very powerful" and "If you make customers unhappy in the physical world, they might each tell 6 friends. If you make customers unhappy on the Internet, they can each tell 6,000 friends." (referralcandy.com, Blog, 69 of the Best Jeff Bezos Quotes, accessed August 20, 2020)

Many companies pay lip service to the above to their own detriment. Here is a classic case story to illustrate this.

Background

The company is www.totalsportshop.com. It was formed in November 2009 and professes to be the Number 1 online football shop in the UK. Orders are placed online via their website and all customer contact is restricted to e-mail only with no telephone contact number.

The case study concerns a female customer who ordered four football kits (shirt, shorts, and socks) for her grandchildren as 2019 Christmas presents. Having searched several sites, she elected to buy from Total Sports because they guaranteed delivery before Christmas, which was obviously an important buying criteria. The order was placed and invoiced on December 2, 2019 with payment made up front.

Customer Experience

The customer experience in sequential order was:

1. E-mail confirming the order was being processed received dated December 5.
2. E-mail confirming the order was being packed received dated December 14.
3. E-mail confirming the order was dispatched received dated December 17. These e-mails provided reassurance that everything was fine.
4. Order delivered on December 20 but incomplete. One set of shirt/shorts and all four pairs of socks missing. E-mail sent to the company on the same day advising company and urgently requesting advice on when missing items will be delivered, emphasizing that these are Christmas presents.
5. Company sent e-mail dated December 21 stating that missing items will be sent out on that day for special delivery on December 22.
6. Items never arrived. Customer had the embarrassment of not being able to give one of her grandchildren a present whilst having to explain to all four about the missing socks.
7. After a busy Christmas period, customer sent e-mail of complaint to the company on December 30 detailing the circumstances and expressing her major disappointment and frustration.
8. Reply from company received dated December 31 with platitudes of apology and stating that it was being followed up with the warehouse.
9. No contact from the company or delivery had been received by January 7. Customer sent e-mail to the company expressing her disbelief on the incompetence of the company and requesting a status update.

10. Company replied dated January 8 stating that warehouse had prepared the missing items and they will be shipped on January 9.

11. No delivery received by January 14. Further e-mail sent to the company by the customer tabling the history of events and stating she had been totally let down and feeling conned by their company having guaranteed delivery for Christmas 2019 and still not completed by January 14.

12. No reply received.

13. Delivery arrived on January 16 but still incomplete. Four pairs of socks ordered and only three delivered with two of them the wrong size.

14. The customer sent e-mail to the company dated January 20 to communicate the position and asking for delivery date for remaining socks.

15. No reply from the company.

16. The customer sent follow-up e-mail dated January 31.

17. The company replied dated January 31 stating that a £5 refund had been issued for the remaining pair of socks.

18. No refund received four weeks later.

Comment:

- No contact name was ever provided by the company. Communication was impersonal with e-mails simply signed off as "TotalSports."
- Compensation was neither asked for nor volunteered.
- It is provided in detail to illustrate how bad customer service can be practiced and the customer experience at the end of such an appalling approach to business.
- A company does not necessarily know who the customer is. For example, whether he or she is an opinion former with a "Twitter" following of 500,000! As such, it is vital a company treats all customers with respect and a high level of responsiveness and not adopt a perceived aloof and dismissive attitude. It may come back to "bite them in the bum!"

*(Sophia Bernazzani, The Ultimate Guide to customer retention, Hubspot Blog, accessed November, 2019), (Hemsley, How customer experience is building brands and business, *Marketing Week*, June 6, 2019), (Innovation PEI- Province of Ontario, Customer Relationship Management, 2013, accessed May 15, 2019), (Lim Eng Kong, Guest satisfaction and guest loyalty study for hotel industry, RIT Scholar Works, accessed July 9, 2020).

Who to Build a Relationship With?

The commercial focus of CRM is to develop a company's "best customers" on the principle that **"All customers are equal but some are more equal than others."**

To identify which customers contribute most to revenue and profit and use their profile to acquire "look-a-like" new customers.

The route to success is through segmentation with customer strategies put in place appropriate to each segment including the level of funding. The central theme is not to treat all customers the same way but to tailor programs reflective of the revenue opportunity and the profile of the customers resident in each segment.

Conceptually, this is simplistically illustrated in Figure 6.4 with objectives aligned to value opportunities.

An extra layer of sophistication can be added by breaking the loyalty/value groups down into more refined segments and introducing a third dimension of recency to build an RFV model (Recency, Frequency,

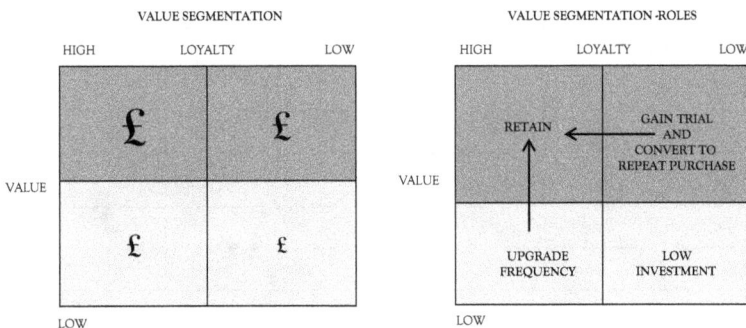

Figure 6.4 Value segmentation translated into action

Value); each segment having a value attributed to it with customer counts. As discussed in Chapter 4, this enhances the ability to efficiently and effectively target, set quantifiable objectives, and measure return on activities. An important element is the ability to identify and isolate customers who are about to lapse and those who have lapsed with communications in place to address each situation, as illustrated in Table 6.1:

Priorities can be ranked by segment, funds allocated, and customer programs structured. So far, the focus has been on behavioral measurements and not picking up on the customer profiles pertinent to each segment. Obviously, this is critical because the content, tone, and style of communication should be honed to the customer characteristics of each segment. Hence, at this juncture, each priority segment should be

Table 6.1 The RFV model

	ACTIVE	SEMI-ACTIVE	LAPSED
ACTIVE LOYALS			
High Spend			
Mid Spend			
Low Spend			
PASSIVE LOYALS			
High Spend			
Mid Spend			
Low Spend			
SPLIT LOYALS			
High Spend			
Mid Spend			
Low Spend			
SHIFTING LOYALS			
High Spend			
Mid Spend			
Low Spend			
SWITCHERS			
High Spend			
Mid/Low Spend			

profiled and further segmented and grouped according to their propensity to purchase and the commonalities of their profiles. For example, geodemographically, there may be a simple split between three groups using CACI's system in the UK as the refereence:

- High ranking best prospects = Acorn Groups A/B
- Medium ranking best prospects = Acorn Groups D/E/J
- Low ranking best prospects = Acorn Groups C/I

Objectives can be set and programs constructed. This approach is illustrated in Figure 6.5 using "High Spending Loyals" as the reference segment.

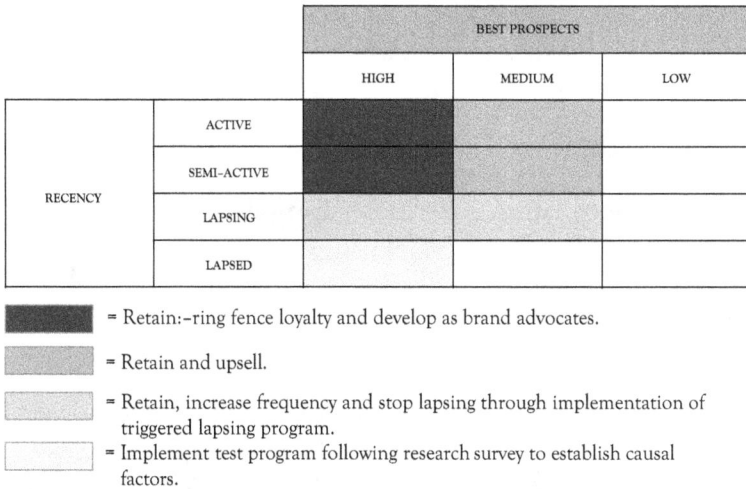

		BEST PROSPECTS		
		HIGH	MEDIUM	LOW
	ACTIVE			
RECENCY	SEMI-ACTIVE			
	LAPSING			
	LAPSED			

= Retain:-ring fence loyalty and develop as brand advocates.

= Retain and upsell.

= Retain, increase frequency and stop lapsing through implementation of triggered lapsing program.

= Implement test program following research survey to establish causal factors.

Figure 6.5 Segmentation model applications based on the "High Spend Loyals" segment

It is self-evident that communications should be bespoke to customer characteristics if the aim is to maximize engagement and response. After all, the more relevant the message, the more chance of it being read and a dialogue ensuing.

For example, millennials are vastly different from the post war "baby boomers."

The millennium shopper has more money, relative to their previous generation counterparts and a greater desire to shop but less time to do it and less inclination to accept the status quo. Judgmentally, their central message can be summarized in three words: Time (save me time), Treasures (give me a pleasant experience), and Trust (let me believe you). Another characteristic is that they have a tendency to change their minds. They are not easy to typecast and the previously used marketing pigeonholes are no longer appropriate.

In contrast, "baby boomers" are rich in terms of time, money, and assets. They are more attitudinally "young" compared to the earlier generations at the same life stage and more active with a big chunk of leisure time. To many sectors, particularly hospitality, these are a highly attractive group with the disposable income and inclination to spend it on quality experiences.

It is readily apparent that "one size does not fit all" and the same communication sent to all customers will be perceived as "junk mail."

In conclusion, segmentation is the "name of the game" with targeting as the theme—who to target, with what and when. Micro marketing and not macro marketing.

How to Build a Relationship—Relationship Marketing

Introduction

In many markets, over time, products converge in terms of their physical characteristics and functional performance. Customers can take these factors for granted and, if so, there is the consequent opportunity to escalate the less tangible, more emotional factors in importance in the purchase decision. In doing so, the route to building a durable customer franchise becomes more dependent on adding value through emotional benefits as a positive brand discriminator. What values can we add apart from the rational values of product features/benefits related to customer wants and lifestyle? If successful, the quality of the customer relationship with a brand will be the ultimate differentiator.

The CRM model enables this to be put into practice by gathering and storing customer information and segmenting the customer universe. This facilitates the ability to build relationships with "best customers"— to nurture the relationship through personalized one-to-one communication thereby building connectivity between brand and customer which, in turn, bonds loyalty.

The task of Relationship Marketing is to build true loyalty in key customer segments. The strategic approach is to build an emotional bridge between the customer and the brand, which builds extra value into the relationship on top of the physical characteristics of the product or service. In so doing, it is positively seeking to change attitudes as a means of changing behavior—of moving target customers to "Active Loyal" status and brand advocacy.

It's about a relationship, not a "one-night stand." Building a long-term relationship using a process of seduction and not bribery.

Like all successful relationships, the more relevant and fresher the content, the better chance of sustaining the relationship. It is analogous to marriage, which is expanded here:

The Relationship Journey

The relationship between a brand and its purchasers is like any relationship between two people. Advertising is akin to the wooing process. Each partner preens themselves, makes sure they look their best, and then approaches the other. Harsh words are never spoken and a rosy view of the future is guaranteed. The process either fails or progresses to the engagement—the first formal indication that the relationship is developing.

Engagement then leads to marriage. Marriage can lead to a life-long commitment and happiness or to a series of pitfalls; trial separations, affairs, divorce. Indeed, marriage so often leads to divorce, that marriage guidance counselling services have sprung up to stem the tide.

Let us briefly explore the steps in this journey, and in so doing, enhance our understanding to ensure that brand loyalty remains intact and the crisis point of divorce is not reached. Figure 6.6 diagrammatically depicts the journey based on a B2C brand.

Courtship

Most brands begin their relationship with a prospective purchaser with a whirlwind courtship. The brand spends a huge amount on advertising and promotion, wooing the trusting purchaser with a dazzling display of wealth and confidence.

But, for most brands, this courtship does not progress into anything meaningful. The initial flood of attention becomes a drip feed and then disappears until the next accounting year. Meanwhile, there is the risk that a rival suitor puffs out its chest, opens its wallet, and goes on the offensive.

Unless you can catch the purchaser before the rival's kiss, you may lose them forever!

Engagement

Many marketers eschew promiscuity and hold out the promise of a long-term relationship through an engagement with the purchaser. This may mean no more than asking for the purchaser's name, address, and a few personal details in response to a promotion offer. Asking for personal details early on in the relationship is like presenting a ring. It implies further commitment, consideration, and attention. Here again, marketers can slip up. Ignoring their catch and leaving the purchaser open to those ever-lurking suitors.

The Wedding

A conventionally managed engagement will be consummated with a wedding, letting the outside world know that a knot has been tied. In the process of customer retention, this is the stage when the purchaser is encouraged to communicate to others their brand advocacy.

However, marketing managers are not necessarily made in heaven. They may flourish as a result of a continued and thoughtful enticement but they may also wither as a result of simply taking the purchaser for granted. Just like real life! Many brands choose bribery to keep purchasers loyal. Coupons and discounts are discourteously thrown at the marriage partner as though they were a prostitute offering themselves for hire. Where a careful and solicitous seduction is not attempted, the resulting decline in the relationship is assured.

Affairs

A purchaser, treated in a promiscuous way by the brand marketer will, sooner or later, react. They will find solace in another bright, new exciting brand, which they will have noticed in-store, online, or in advertising, finding it hard to resist temptation. They're on the slippery slope.

Trial Separation

Suitors will bombard the distressed purchaser with promotions and loyalty schemes to force a trial separation from your brand. All too often, they succeed.

Divorce

The purchaser tires of waiting for your brand to repair the damage, change your ways, and behave appealingly. They move in with a suitor brand or they opt for the free and easy life of promiscuity.

Happy Marriage

This slippery slope to broken bonds and purchaser desertion is not generated by the purchaser but by the behavior of the brand. We could behave differently. There are simple rules to a happy relationship with a purchaser just as there are to a harmonious marriage.

The solution to the relationship breakdown is to employ the process of customer relationship marketing. To build interactive relationships between the brand and the individual customer, which directly impact attitudes as a means of influencing behavior. This is best achieved by fully utilizing all the information held on a customer marketing database.

In summary, reinforcing points previously made, the keys to a long-lasting, loyal, and successful relationship are twofold:

1. We need to understand the functional needs and emotional wants of our customers to help explain the way they behave and how they make their purchasing decisions. We can then translate this understanding into a benefit-led proposition, talking to our purchaser in the right way so that they find the relationship satisfying.
2. Building a robust data strategy (what kind of data is most useful to us, how to collect it, how do we analyze it) with a customer centric database at its heart.

Introduction
(Right person, permission, right name)

↓

Courtship
(Process of seduction begins)

↓

Engagement/Living Together
(Process of sharing information begins)

↓

The Wedding/Joint Mortgage

Affairs
(Lower price alternatives)

Nurturing
(Relationship established –
advocacy follows)

Trial Separation
(Brand Switching)

Mutual Development
(Sharing friends' names)

Divorce
(Left Home)

Lifetime Involvement
(The fruits of loyalty)

Key factors: appeal, choice, dialogue, attention, mutuality, trust, emotional engagement, and commitment

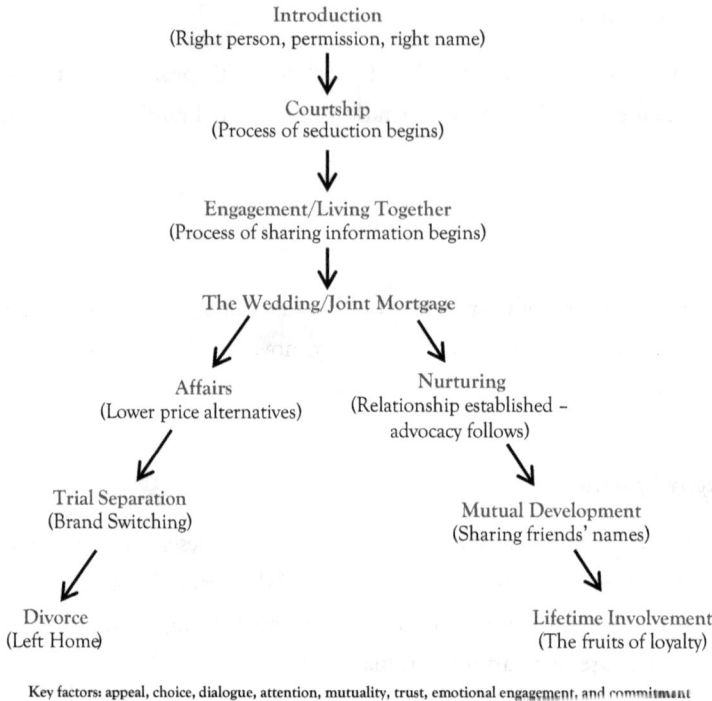

Figure 6.6 The relationship journey

Rules of Engagement

The key success factors for engaging "best practice" customer relationship marketing are:

1. Knowledge is power. Really understand customer needs, wants, and purchase motivations alongside their life stage and lifestyle profiles.
2. Segmentation is key with concentration on priority segments. Identify "best customers"—those who meet the commercial criteria of who you want to build a relationship with.
3. Develop relationships only with customers who actively wish to participate.
4. Develop a clear, cohesive creative strategy enshrined in a brand positioning statement with the brand proposition at the center.
5. Add demonstrable value to the brand through the program.
6. **As with any relationship, seduction is lasting, bribery is temporary. Do not "sell" to the customer. The communication should**

be welcomed and engaged, resulting in a dialogue being triggered.

7. Build trust and never abuse it. The customer provides data and trusts that it will be used effectively to communicate relevant messages. They further trust that their data will be securely kept and never sold to third parties. Never betray customer confidence.

8. Develop brand affection. The loyal customer respects the brand to the extent they believe the brand is looking after their interests and the information they receive is accurate and honest.

9. The impact of customer relationship marketing programs is not judged by the response rate to a single mailing but by the change in attitudes and related behavior over a 2–3 year period.

10. Correspondence should be personal—not mass mailing by nature. Contact must always be personal, inclusive, and intimate.

11. The relationship must be nurtured and never taken for granted. At all times, the brand must develop an emotional bonding by ensuring that key customer groups feel pampered and privileged. Treat customers like friends/colleagues. Talk with them and avoid use of formality.

12. Loyalty is clearly a strategic and long-term issue, and yet, the most frequent mechanism chosen for its development is quick fix bribery. Beware of the pitfalls.

13. Set milestone goals and monitor against them. If objectives change, adjust the program accordingly.

14. Customer Relationship Marketing focuses on direct contact with the customer; showing them we know and understand their needs and wants, even before they are aware of them! In this respect, an important principle is to show customers we are receptive to their changing lifestyles and needs and wants. This potentially means a constant evolution of communication methods and contents.

Key Success Factors

1. Recognize from the beginning that it is a strategic tool, which can involve substantial set-up costs. Buy into this and show long-term commitment with payback over a 2+ year period.

2. Put in place clear, quantifiable, and measurable objectives from the outset.
3. Get sign off at the most senior level in the organization.
4. Appoint a Customer Relationship Marketing champion.
5. Fully integrate into the fabric of the overall sales and marketing strategy and plans. Clearly allocate budgets for the Customer Relationship Marketing program with precise timings.
6. Implement effective measurement systems with focus on ROI.
7. Integrate with all the relevant internal functions who potentially interface with customers who are members of the program, including customer services.
8. Putting in place creative partners who have the art direction and copy skills to translate the creative strategy into superb execution with the sensitivities required to build personal relationships.

When to Consider Customer Relationship Marketing

The technique is appropriate to companies where the central objective is to build or protect customer loyalty; particularly with "best customers" who account for a substantial proportion of company revenue and profit, as the principal means of building and securing long-term profitability.

Typically, the product or service will have some or all of the following characteristics:

1. A highly competitive category where the consumer has a choice from a portfolio of brands. For example, Spirits, Supermarkets, Lager, Casual Dining Restaurants, Insurance, Wine Retailers (on and off line), Retail Banking, Cars.
2. Where differences in functional benefits between brands in the product/service category are marginal thereby potentially placing extra emphasis on emotional benefits to determine positive consumer brand selection. For example, retail banking, insurance, supermarkets, malt whisky, DIY retailers, sportswear.
3. Where the market category is mature and the "80:20" rule applies with a large heavy user group—20 percent of category consumers

being "heavy" users accounting for 80 percent of category volume. Maximizing brand loyalty amongst the heavy user group is therefore the key to improving profitability. In parallel, the brand may already draw the bulk of its sales from regular buyers of whom an important proportion are very loyal where the priority is to protect sales.

4. The category exhibits a high frequency purchase cycle facilitating the opportunity for a brand to develop more intimate relationships and emotional bonding.

5. Where the brand intrinsically possesses a number of characteristics capable of placing it in a niche.

6. For corporate brands with the opportunity to cross sell across a portfolio of products/services on the back of the first product/service purchased. For example, retail banks, building societies, insurance brokers, hotel groups, airlines, insurance companies, holiday companies.

7. In categories where a low frequency cycle is counteracted by a high unit price/margin and emotional benefits can be an important part of the sales proposition. For example, cars and holiday companies.

8. Where the target consumer audience is segmented into identifiable clusters with specific characteristics and needs/wants.

9. Where there is commercial logic in influencing attitudes to change behavior by targeting individuals with high quality personalized communication rather than by reaching them through more mass market media channels.

Case Studies

1. **How not to do it**

   I received 20 e-mails over a period of 9 weeks in the Spring and Autumn of 2019 from John Lewis; a premier department store retailer in Great Britain. They all followed a similar format summarized as follows:

   - Built to a common formula with a lead category/product with other featured product categories following as you scroll down. The products featured did not form part of an integrated theme and were mainly unrelated. The reader had no awareness of what's to follow and how long the journey will take.

- The creative format was common to all. They used stylish, well cropped product settings with simple, clear lines. Photography was of a high quality standard.
- Primary messaging was promotion led with a "Price Match" message always present.
- They are best described as being sales-led; being dominated by promotion activity.
- In summary, it was a good format for a sales-led, product portfolio approach with classy, well presented products.

However, it did not fall under the umbrella of Customer Relationship Marketing with the following negatives:

- The bold message on the e-mails I received stated: "This e-mail has no content." There was no personalization; either by name or message. It was obviously a mass e-marketing campaign across their customer database.
- Apart from it being impersonal, the products featured were not relevant to me either in terms of my purchase history or my geodemographic profile.
- The approach was decidedly not customer friendly.

In all probability, the main objective behind the campaign was to generate short term sales given the dire trading conditions experienced across the UK high street in 2019. However, it undermined my respect for the John Lewis brand and the trust and confidence I had in their professionalism in which it always seemed to me that they placed their customers on a pedestal. The impersonal, junk e-mail nature of the communications did not sit comfortably with the brand image I had built up over many years of spending a shed load of money with them. Surely, they were able to recognize the virtues of "best practice" one-to-one marketing and go the extra yard of adding my name with a personal message; perhaps expressed through their desire to share with me some excellent sales opportunities they had in store!

2. **How to do it**

A case study based on the UK Port market.

Port Market Situation

1. Port brands had similar product characteristics, sourced from the same wine growing region in Portugal and all had a good heritage and pedigree. Brands such as Warre's, Dow's, Cockburn, Taylor's, and Graham's. There was an absence of product differentiators and brand USPs.

2. Brands tended to concentrate their consumer communication spend in the run up to Christmas; the most expensive time to advertise and to achieve brand awareness and recognition in a crowded market. Spend levels were limited and any awareness built soon evaporated with a high advertising decay factor.

3. All consumers were treated the same as a uniform mass in receiving the same communication.

4. In depth analysis of the buying universe revealed significant consumer segmentation with a major bias to a heavy user group. The heavy user segment accounted for 15 percent of buyers but 60 percent of bottle volume. On average, they bought 6 bottles a year; that is, a bottle every 8 weeks. They bought year round and not just at Christmas, when they tended to also buy Port to give as a gift. In contrast, light buyers bought an average of 1 bottle per year accounting for 58 percent of buyers but only 17 percent of volume.

   In addition, within the heavy user segment, there was an inner core of 200,000 "super heavy buyers" accounting for 2.5 percent of category buyers but 23 percent of volume; buying, on average, 17.5 bottles per year.

5. The heavy user segment had a very distinctive profile:
   - Their geodemographic profile was skewed toward Acorn Groups A (Lavish Lifestyles), B (Executive Wealth), C (Mature Money), D (City Sophisticates), and E (Career Climbers) based on CACI's geodemographic system in the UK.
   - Consumers enjoyed high incomes—in the top 10 percent of income earners at their particular life stage.

- They were discerning and discriminating in their lifestyle choices.
- Socializing was high on their agenda in which food and wine formed an integral part. Hosting and participating in supper parties with friends and family was the norm with conversation over a glass of port at the end of the meal being a regular theme.
- They had a high affection for Port with a thirst for knowledge.

The challenge was how to boost volume and market share in the above market framework.

Solution

One of the brands (Brand X) took up the challenge by engaging a Customer Relationship Marketing process embodying the following strategic strands:

1. Target audience of the heavy user segment in Acorn Groups A/B/C/D/E.
2. Put in place a data capture protocol defining the data to be captured in all the recruitment activities covering:
   - Personal details including full address, e-mail address, gender, and DOB
   - Port brands drunk and also purchased to give as a gift by loyalty category—only, most often, sometimes and never
   - Number of bottles bought per year for self-consumption and to give as a gift
   - Usual price paid
   - Source of purchase
   - Opt-in to receiving communication
3. Recruitment was conducted through in-pack promotions, direct mail to lists of known port drinkers, and promotions in conjunction with a radio station with a complementary audience profile. In each case, the free offer was to receive "A Booklet about Port"—a wry look at some of the colorful history and traditions of port with wonderful cartoons and tasting notes. The recruitment target criteria was set at buying two or more bottles per year and consumers who did not meet this were filtered out at this stage and did not receive future communications.

4. The creative property developed was under the theme of "Tales to tell over supper"; in which communication to target members of the customer database featured a little book with a different tale from the vineyard and the people who make the port. This was the emotional bridge built between the consumers and the brand on which the consumers were on the inside track with intimate knowledge shared with them—who, in turn, could relay the stories over their supper parties.

5. Strict creative guidelines were laid down, which must be adhered to at all times.

6. Two mailings were sent per year plus a uniquely designed Christmas card with a poem. Personalized direct mail was used as the communication medium and always featured a postage stamp designed to absolutely avoid any linkage to "junk mail." This medium was deliberately used to build a personal, more intimate relationship.

7. No coupons were used. A Free Prize Draw for a selection of Port was featured in every mailing generating a response of 30+ percent—with some over 40 percent—with the winners' names featured in the next mail reinforcing the transparency and honesty of the program. Participation was very strong to the extent that mail collections were featured on "eBay."

8. A mail survey to the database elicited a 25 percent response. The questionnaire mirrored the one used on recruitment to enable changes in behavior to be measured against the year they were recruited. This showed a demonstrable upward shift in consumption and enabled ROI calculations to be made with a significant positive return.

9. External market panel data showed a 33 percent share gain in the heavy user segment whilst the economic benefits of the program enabled savings to be made in other parts of the marketing budget.

Steps to Take

The following steps should be undertaken in determining a customer loyalty strategy:

1. Conduct an audit to build a robust, comprehensive picture of your customer knowledge covering, for example:
   - Segment market by usage and define brand status relative to other brands within the overall market category and within each segment. Quantify source of volume in total and by brand by segment identifying opportunities and areas requiring protection.
   - Features and benefits of all competing brands.
   - Needs, wants, and purchase motivations of category and brand buyers in total and any variations by segment.
   - Identify current status of customer database including quality, quantity, and sources—data held, where and how it's held, how it's collected, accuracy, compliance with data protection laws in the operating region(s), and so on.
   - Understand the current data capture protocol(s).
   - Segment database by recency, frequency, and value.
2. From the above:
   a. Build value segments and identify target behavior adopting the central principle that customers are not created equally in terms of potential profit and should not be treated as if they were. In so doing, define what is needed to drive positive behavior change.
   b. Strategy development:
      - Who to target. Identify target audience describing them on all relevant attributes. In particular, what are their attitudes and purchase motivations. In so doing, realistically identify whether you can meet their expectations or whether fundamental product/service improvements are required.
      - Embellish the targeting by adding the dimension of potential spend with a focus on increasing "share of wallet"—that is, what they spend with you is not necessarily what they have available to spend.
      - Identify target behavior patterns for each segment.
      - Define your benefit-led product/service proposition and brand positioning relative to the needs and wants you are going to address.

- Build the business model to quantify targets, how much you have to invest, and payback criteria.

c. Program branding. Loyalty program must be intrinsically linked to the brand values. Translate brand positioning into a creative strategy and execution for the loyalty program with focus on what you are selling and how you are going to communicate it.

d. Communication planning. What communications will drive the desired positive behavioral change:

- How are you going to reach new customers and what is the cost of acquisition?
- How are you going to build a relationship with customers on the database and what is the cost of doing so?

e. Database development. This is a key aspect because the database should effectively act as the marketing partner, which, if built and engaged properly, will:

- Trigger the right communication to the right target at the right time.
- Feed in all the contact information from all the sources.
- Deliver the ability to market to the individual thereby underpinning the principles of relationship building.
- Ensure information is collected from all the contact points and held in a consistent form against each customer on the database. This has the additional benefit of enabling straightforward modelling of "like-minded" customers using, for example, simple regression.

To do so, the following check list is a top-line guide:

- Identify your customer data gaps and how, if at all, you are going to fill them.
- Lay down your future data capture protocol.
- Specify any improvements required to the functionality of the customer centric database, how they are going to be made with timings and cost.

- Identify all the future data collection points, how data will be collected and transferred to the database.
- Put in place a data processing manual.

3. Set up a system to measure, monitor, and evaluate including the following:
   - Set clear quantified strategic objectives from the outset
   - Build measurement tools and reporting systems up front
   - Establish an inviolate control group to allow you to go back and add an extra dimension to the evaluation of investment decisions
   - Act on results—roll out winners and kill losers

Loyalty Programs

The manifestation of loyalty is repeat purchasing by existing customers. There are two types of marketing mechanics that companies can deploy to potentially help deliver this objective; one coming under the heading of promotion and the other as loyalty programs.

The Promotion Approach

This approach uses the promotion mechanic of sending coupons to all the members of its customer database and/or offering price discounts either in the form of a straightforward X percent off or bonus offers such as "2 for the price of 1." Codes can be used to track redemption by individual customer.

This route is classical promotion territory and nobody should be under the illusion that it constitutes a loyalty program. It is using blatant bribery to "buy" loyalty, which is the impossible dream. You have to earn loyalty. This approach potentially results in one or more of the following:

- It mortgages business by bringing purchase forward. This applies to the situations where consumption levels will not change because of usage frequency profiles; for example, household cleaning products or toiletries. Therefore, the only financial gain is if it blocks competitors. Otherwise, it is simply reducing margins.

- It encourages promiscuity; primarily appealing to "shifting loyals" or "switchers." You can identify such customers on the customer database if you track redemptions using coupon codes with a customer URN. A purchase pattern clearly emerges where such customers only buy on promotion. If so, couponing should be restricted to those customers on the database who respond to such promotions and deployed when and if there is a need to generate short term volume.
- It can undermine loyalty for the remaining customers on the database who are probably the most important contributors to profit. They have a negative perception of always being "sold to" in a very impersonal way. They do not feel special.
- The bonus program could potentially be justified if customer information is collected as a byproduct of the activity. "It is the price I pay for the information I get." However, it should be commissioned with your "eyes open" because you are buying knowledge through it and not loyalty.

Loyalty Programs

These are programs where the loyalty scheme is an integral part of the brand's makeup and is fully embraced in the customer offering. It is used as a brand discriminator to encourage positive brand selection. The primary difference here is that the brand is rewarding customer loyalty. They are not paying for the membership of the club. They are being rewarded for their custom—the more they use the brand, the more reward benefits they earn.

The most successful and high profile examples of this approach in the UK is Tesco Clubcard and British Airways Avios. Both schemes have the additional benefits of collecting very rich customer information. They are in possession of comprehensive customer information both in terms of their buying behavior and their personal profiles. We know "knowledge is power" and both brands have this in abundance with the ability to use it to maximum commercial gain. In such schemes, some guidelines to take on board are:

- Do not over reward. For example, one of the outcomes of Tesco's Clubcard testing program was that a 1 percent reward level generated a similar response to a 2 percent level.
- Ensure the core benefits and brand proposition are relevant, up-to-date and provide clear differential reasons for the customer to buy the product/service. Remember, the loyalty program is an integral part of the brand's customer offering. It is the brand's total offering that delivers loyalty—not just the loyalty program itself.
- Validate that the purchase frequency cycle is compatible with the loyalty scheme's mechanics and rewards to ensure maximum participation levels.
- Model any liabilities of the program way ahead.
- Avoid insincere communications. Make sure the scheme is totally transparent and honest in everything it does.
- Remember, active loyalty is measured by the actual redemption of the rewards and not by the rewards earned.
- Ensure the scheme is fully supported by staffing and processes to deliver best practice customer service experience at all customer touch points.
- Communication should be rooted in the principles of Relationship Marketing.
- Customer data is the key to truly intelligent loyalty schemes. By embracing data capture as a central part of a loyalty scheme, you will benefit from two key things that are essential to keeping customers loyal—connection and relevance. Stay connected with your customers at a frequency in line with the purchase cycle and, in so doing, provide **relevant** and personalized content, offers, and promotions. The central ethos is to engage with customers and build a relationship—not to simply "sell" to them. The more you use the data captured to do so, the better chance of building the "relationship bridge."

Some Key Thoughts to Reflect on if You Are Considering/Reviewing CRM

Cementing customer loyalty is the route to sustainable long-term profitability. But what is loyalty and how do we go about developing an umbilical cord tying the customer to the brand?

We focused on intimately and comprehensively knowing your customer in Chapter 5. If you follow the guidelines laid down, you will know your customer's needs and wants and the extent to which your brand satisfies them relative to the competing brands. This is "base camp" in your quest to climb the customer loyalty mountain.

From there, you need to convert that knowledge into building an ongoing relationship with your "best customers." To lock them into purchasing your brand in preference to other brand choices, thereby optimizing your "share of wallet" and leveraging CLV (Customer Lifetime Value). This is probably one of the biggest but most difficult marketing challenges and yet is often given the least priority by many marketers as they concentrate their energies more on acquisition of new customers than retention of the existing ones.

The first and fundamental step is to recognize and quantify the importance of customer retention to your brand's revenue and profit. Once you understand the financial equation, you will "buy into" the commercial role and importance of customer retention to your business and approach the development of customer loyalty with enthusiasm and vision. Indeed, you should adopt the mantle of the loyalty evangelist and "lead the company to the promised land" by communicating its importance throughout the company.

Thereafter, in pursuing the loyalty challenge, you should follow the thought processes illustrated in this chapter and use it as your checklist in developing the customer loyalty part of your CRM strategy.

The key elements are:

1. Ask yourself two basic questions:
   - Why is loyalty important?
   - What is loyalty?

It is vital you can understand these because they underpin the concept of customer loyalty. You are then in a position to communicate internally and with external partners with passion and knowledge because you have a fundamental grasp of the concept whilst relating it to your own brand situation. There are four important strands of thought in addressing these questions:

- "All customers are equal but some are more equal than others." The Pareto principle applies to most brands with a small proportion of customers accounting for a disproportionate level of revenue. Quantify the ratio pertaining to your brand and identify who they are.
- Loyalty is a strategic issue. It is not a one-off marketing activity. It relates to defining a customer's lifetime value and the incremental revenue that can be generated by increasing your "share of wallet." Have you done the calculation for your brand?
- In many mature markets, brands tend to converge in the features and benefits they offer whilst, in parallel, there can be a growing overall level of consumer fatigue. In this context, it must be accepted that you cannot buy loyalty—you have to earn it. The challenge can be one of identifying differential emotional benefits in tune with the attitude systems, mood, and lifestyle of your target audience.
  You should therefore ask yourself the basic question: does your company genuinely and thoroughly track customer needs/wants and adjust the physical characteristics of the product/service and its brand proposition and positioning accordingly?
- Loyalty measurement is not one dimensional. It must take into account the reasons behind their observed purchase behavior.
  In reality, there is a profound difference between attitudinal loyalty and behavioral loyalty and, in the context of the latter, degrees of loyalty as measured by your share of customer expenditure on the total category.

- Do you acknowledge this in your company and, secondly, do you quantify measurement on all customer dimensions with particular focus on developing market research techniques to investigate attitudes, perceptions, and motivations linked to purchase behavior?

2. Once you have these central themes locked into your thinking, this chapter helps you move into action mode in two particular ways:

   - Building your customer segmentation model to identify and profile your "best prospects" to target your customer loyalty development against. Importantly, how you translate such segmentation models into a communication program.

   - Introduction to the process of Relationship Marketing as the primary route in thinking through and executing a program to develop customer loyalty.

3. This chapter finally ends on the subject of loyalty programs. In this context, you need to question whether your brand fundamentals are compatible with a loyalty program and, if so, what the payback would be. You need to answer this with total objectivity and not be seduced by the technology of the loyalty apps being marketed (which can look so appealing).

CHAPTER 7

The "M" in CRM*

The Macro Picture

Bluntly put, CRM technology is all about managing a company's customer relationships. That is why many people think CRM is technology led. But, CRM technology is not the tail wagging the CRM dog!

The customer first
The CRM strategy second
The CRM systems solution third

The CRM philosophy is simple—PUT THE CUSTOMER FIRST. It is a customer centric business model. It starts and ends with the customer. There are some famous quotes by Jeff Bezos of Amazon to reinforce this:

"It's our customers who tell us what to do next."

"The most important single thing is to focus obsessively on the customer. Our goal is to be the earth's most customer-centric company."

(refferralcandy, blog, 69 of the Best Jeff Bezos Quotes, accessed August 20, 2020)

> The CRM strategy is forged against a customer focus. It is a top-down business model. It is strategy driven—not process driven.
> *Strategy first, how to deliver it second. Business first, technology second.*
> *The CRM strategy places the customer at the center of everything you do. CRM systems help turn the strategy into reality.*

No technology, no matter how sophisticated, can be successful without a strategy to guide its purpose, its implementation, and its use. CRM strategy and technology must work together in harness in order to bring a customer centric plan to life.

In this context, CRM systems play an absolutely pivotal role in delivering the CRM strategy through managing a company's relationships and interactions with customers and potential customers. It helps companies stay connected to customers, streamline processes, and ultimately improve profitability. In parallel, it helps to enhance and enrich the customer experience at every touch point with the company because, when a business looks at every transaction through the eyes of the customer, it cannot help but deliver a better customer experience which, in turn, helps cement loyalty to the company.

CRM software aligns sales, marketing, and customer service departments together. By putting the customer first, separate data silos are broken down to become unified under one roof to reflect a customer centric company. CRM software knits together all the data from different departments throughout the company to give one, singular holistic view of each customer in real time.

It allows a company to orchestrate all the customer contact activities to deliver a consistently personalized, differentiated customer experience regardless of the interactive channel chosen by the customer with a common experience witnessed at all the touch points with the company. This enables companies to merge together marketing, sales and customer service functions under a single communications umbrella, thereby avoiding the outcome of disparate messaging coming from traditional methods where contact communication was often pursued in separate, ad-hoc ways. The result is a more comprehensive, scientific, methodical approach to identifying, converting, and retaining the most valuable customers.

Furthermore, it empowers customer facing employees in areas such as marketing, sales, and customer service to make quick and informed decisions on everything from up-selling and cross-selling to improving the quality of customer communication and responsiveness to coordinating and evaluating communication campaigns.

CRM software pulls all the customer related data into one central customer centric database. Data from sources such as communication to and from customers (via e-mail, telephone, website, social media, post, etc.), transaction data, surveys, and automatically migrates other information such as customers' personal preferences on communication channels. In so doing, it totally supports a customer centric strategy through data management and automation, as conceptually shown in Figure 7.1.

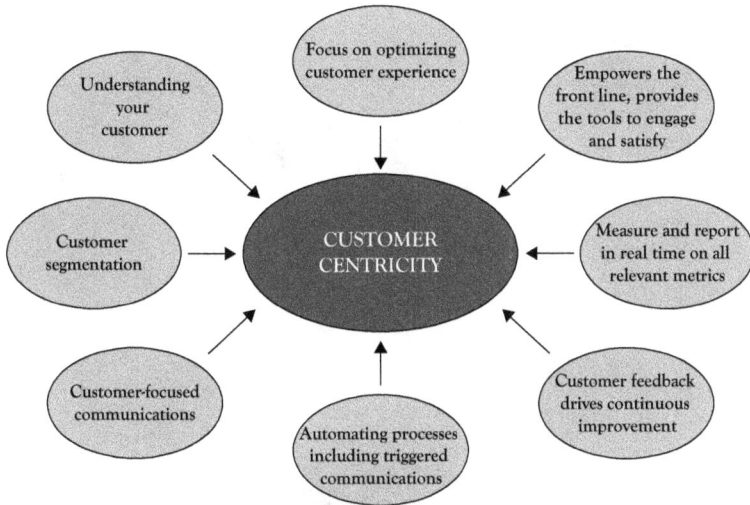

Figure 7.1 The influence of a customer centric strategy

The CRM system then organizes the information to give users a complete record of individuals and companies with everything seen in one place—a simple customizable dashboard that can tell users a customer's previous transaction and response history, their order status, and outstanding issues for B2B, and so on. This enables a business to deepen its relationships with customers. Forging good relationships and keeping track of prospects and customers is critical for customer acquisition and retention and this rests at the core of the CRM functionality. To facilitate this, every transaction should ideally be attributed with a date and unique reference thereby helping to identify loyalty and engagement levels.

CRM software improves customer relationship management by creating a 360 degree view of the customer as diagrammatically shown in Figure 7.2. It enables users to record, report, and analyze customer interactions with the company and presents the information in a readily accessible and usable way.

Importantly, since a CRM system centralizes all customer facing information into a single data silo, finger pointing and discussions on having a common understanding of data definitions are significantly reduced.

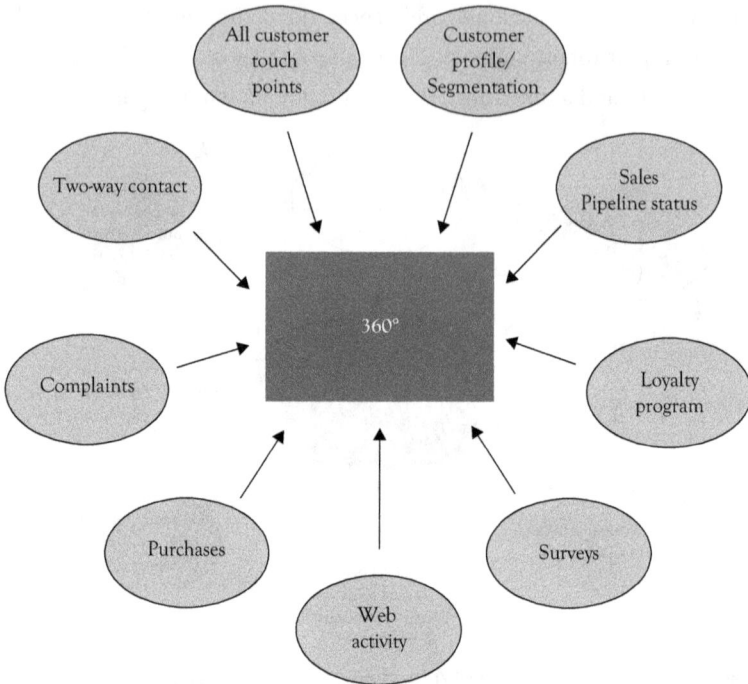

Figure 7.2 360 degree view of the customer

Barriers encouraging a "blame game" culture are removed. Everyone has the same access to the same customer information giving a 360 degree customer view.

One vital ingredient in the CRM mix for CRM systems is its ability to enhance customer experience, which is intrinsically linked to developing good customer relationships. Every time a customer comes in contact with a company, through any communication channel, the customer has the opportunity to form an opinion—be it good, bad, or indifferent. Over time, their collective set of experiences forms a picture in their mind, which, in turn, helps shape their image of the company/brand and its values. CRM systems have the ability to recognize this and fully take on board because we know a poor experience is a step toward customer churn whereas a good experience builds goodwill and encourages related loyalty.

The central tenet of the CRM system is a data driven solution with a single customer view at the middle of the data universe.

A single customer view enables the company to identify the customer across interactions and transaction points facilitating a deeper understanding of how customers engage across channels and the evolving journey to purchase and beyond. Utopia—communications and offers can be tailored to customer behavior patterns and the channels of communication they prefer, thereby strengthening the company's customer connectivity and building deeper loyalty.

Importantly, when customer data across data silos, sources, and channels is connected and is made accessible in real time via a single platform, companies can see not only the level of engagement across each channel at the customer level, but also the effectiveness of each campaign—taking much of the "guesswork" out of campaign optimization decisions with the data informing users, for example, which individuals redeem a specific offer.

This underlines the premise that when data is used in a meaningful way, it results in better customer retention, higher conversion rates, and an improved lifetime value. But it all starts with connecting data to a single customer view.

CRM System Features

There are two aspects to consider: what functions the systems' perform and how is the functionality applied?

Functions

- Collecting data from all the customer data capture points including communication to and from (customer responses) the customers.
- Storing data securely in a customer centric data warehouse giving a single customer view. This includes the functionality for an electronic library to store open text notes from meetings and calls, and so on.
- Organizing customer data in a relational format to ensure efficient data processing and extraction for communication campaigns and data analysis.

- Making all relevant data available and readily accessible to all the user groups in a manner bespoke to their needs; particularly those directly interfacing with the customer.
- Analytical tools to be able to "slice and dice" data to extract maximum benefit in generating insights to enhance decision making.
- Easy and flexible extraction of data based on multi-variable selection criteria using any combination of the data fields held.
- Ability to build and hold customer segments.
- Campaign automation functionality.
- Tracking and reporting of results. Sophisticated reporting capability including graphical presentation of results. Reporting on all the KPI's and designated metrics with facility for real time reporting. As such, reports generated with up-to-date information incorporating revenue forecasting and trend analysis.
- Giving all the users direct 24/7 access to their data from anywhere with an internet connection.

Applications

a. Identifying and tracking potential customers.
b. Marketing applications:
   - Build customer segmentation models and related programs and manage their execution.
   - Campaign management and evaluation.
   - Send customized communication both in terms of content and messaging.
   - Organize triggered communications to enhance marketing efforts at different points in the relationship with customers. For example, lapsing or lapsed.
   - Underpin targeted marketing approach to optimize the allocation of funds against priority objectives in a hierarchy from "best profitable customers" down.
   - Tracking customer activity to derive valuable behavior insights.

- Tracking lead generation with funneling of leads to the relevant internal department/individual to process and convert.

c. Sales team applications:

  - Handling and tracking the sales process from the initial lead to genuine prospect status to quantified sales opportunity to final order conversion.
  - Sales pipeline status.
  - Streamlines the sales process. By being able to visualize the sales pipeline, sales reps can identify the deals that require immediate focus and/or offer the most valuable opportunities.
  - Enables sales personnel to manage their diaries and schedule activity—calls, follow-ups, meetings, taking notes, send invoices, and so on—which enhances efficiency but ensures all opportunities stay on the radar screen and they are not overlooked.
  - Running reports and forecasts.
  - Tracking customer interactions.
  - Builds up a customer knowledge bank thereby ensuring all information stays in the business and does not leave with any key sales personnel departing.

d. Customer Service team applications:

  - Helps to manage service delivery from pre-ordering to contract delivery to post sale nurturing to renewal.
  - Stores customer preferences and tracks all activities associated with them. For example, do not want to receive weekly e-mails.
  - Manages and monitors any post sale interactions.
  - Really adds value to customer experience with customer service having all information at their "finger tips," thereby being able to handle all complaints and queries professionally and with a personal slant.
  - Reduces or, perhaps, eliminates the more tedious aspects of the customer service job releasing time to focus on the customer interface.

e. Workflow automation helping to optimize processes by streamlining mundane workloads, which will be further enhanced in the future by "artificial intelligence (AI)." This enables employees to focus on the more creative and proactive tasks that add value to a customer relationship. In addition to automating tasks, AI will identify buying patterns as the basis for predicting future behavior.

f. The analytics capability helps create better customer satisfaction rates and identify sales opportunities by analyzing customer data to create targeted marketing campaigns. This leads to improved revenue streams.

g. Connectivity through API or FTP connections to handle direct data transfers from data capture points and, where relevant, outward to other databases/data centers or mailing transmission services, either electronic or postal.

CRM System Benefits

Data is the epicenter of CRM systems and, as Bill Gates (salesforce.com, accessed April 23, 2019) once famously said:

"How you gather, manage and use information will determine whether you win or lose."

Benefits flow from the CRM system's design to house and supply data in an easily accessible and usable format to the users to enhance their decision making and manage customer relationships to "best practice" standards of professionalism.

Some of the key benefits are summarized below:

1. Sales management are empowered with a tool kit to perform at the top of their game. From lead generation and onwards through the chain with the ability to manage their pipeline better. This includes the facility to be able to identify and categorize leads by using, for example, a traffic light system.

2. Forecasting accuracy improves from more comprehensive, timely, and quantified data being available.

3. The quality and personalization of customer service is enhanced by customer service teams being able to track conversations across

channels and having customer contact history and profile information available at the touch of a button.

4. Automated work flows and processing translates into a higher level of productivity and employee motivation stemming from the removal of mundane procedures from their job coupled with having the toolkit to perform to a higher level.

5. Cross team collaboration through integration ensuring everyone is "singing off the same hymn sheet." All the users are working from a common data set, thereby removing discussions on data definitions and clearly specifying everyone's responsibilities and accountabilities in the customer relationship chain from lead generation though conversion to ongoing customer development.

6. By capturing relevant customer information, storing it, and analyzing it, strategies and programs can be formulated to:

   • Build a customer segmentation model and, in so doing, identify "best customers" in terms of revenue and profit— current and potential.

   • Employ targeted marketing methodology with objectives set in ranking order by segment and programs developed to deliver them. Campaigns tailored by segment with relevant content, crafted messages, and promotions to reflect any differences in customer profiles and their needs and wants.

   • Funds are prioritized and allocated, based on "hard data," against quantified objectives and customer profitability. Not all customers are equal. For example, some are a drain on the customer service teams despite buying very little. In contrast, some buy frequently, buy new products and services and are strong influencers in their market. CRM helps prioritize sales and marketing efforts against the profit return when dealing with different customer segments.

   • Increased opportunities for cross-selling and up-selling are identified from an improved understanding of customers. There is also the scope to increase referrals from existing customers because of heightened customer service and satisfaction.

- Campaigns and related spend can be fully and properly evaluated with ROI. Campaign tracking provides actionable insights into what type of marketing works for which type of customer, making it easier for marketers to maximize their budgets and deliver greater ROI.
- Anticipating customer needs and wants and aligning products and services and related communication accordingly gives the best chance to win and retain repeat business through increased customer satisfaction. Gathering information from different sources gives unprecedented insight into how customers feel and what they are saying about a company.
- Compiling data into a single customer view enables a company to identify customers across a wide spectrum of interactions set alongside transaction moments (via multiple channels of contact—e-mail, SMS messages, loyalty app, Wi-Fi, online, social media, etc.) giving a deeper understanding of precisely how the customer engages across channels, with their preferred ones, in the evolving pathway to purchase and beyond.
- Companies can see not only the level of engagement across each channel at the customer level, but the effectiveness of each campaign, thereby taking the guesswork out of campaign optimization decisions. Audience and targeting decisions can be based on the combinations most likely to drive transactions and engagement.

The combination of the above factors potentially result in three major commercial benefits:

- Repeat business, customer retention, and loyalty are maximized and translated into improved revenues and customer profitability.
- Marketing efficiency and effectiveness are heightened with response levels boosted alongside optimizing cost of reaching customers through top notch targeting culminating in reduced cost per response. Taking a data driven approach to marketing produces more

successful promotions whilst saving money in the process.

- Leveraging data efficiently can provide a competitive advantage—knowing who your customers are, what products they prefer, how often they buy and engage with the company whilst harnessing all the data into a single customer view. Tesco is the best example of putting these words into action.

7. Profit management is "top of class" because of the following factors:
   - Customer profitability is center stage. This is a step up because, after all, the customer is responsible for the revenue (demand) side of the P & L. Hitherto, many companies primarily reported at the product and/or departmental levels. This pitched profit reporting at the macro level and did not provide a comprehensive, micro picture of how customers were behaving.
   - Sophisticated analytics and reporting across all KPIs and key sales and marketing metrics. Moreover, reporting is accurate, timely, and in real time enabling faster decision making for any actions to be taken reflecting any sensitivity shown by the data.
   - Automation of work flows enhances productivity.
   - Forecasting accuracy is accentuated through better sales pipeline management and provision of accurate data across all customer demand variables.

8. Supply chain, procurement, and partner management teams can manage relationships better.

CRM System Solution—Specification

The most critical task, in determining the CRM system's solution that best fits your requirements and budget, is to write a comprehensive system's functional specification with all the "t's crossed and i's dotted." This, in turn, acts as your formal briefing document to all potential external systems' suppliers.

The steps to follow, culminating in the specification, are as follows:

Conduct a Data Audit and Establish Current Status

Status of Data Currently Held

a. Identify all the current data capture points for the collection of customer data.

b. For each one, identify the following:
   - Data fields captured with any historical changes by timing point.
   - Contact status under Data Protection Laws in all relevant countries in which you are operating.
   - How data is captured and at which frequency?
   - Where is the data stored and how is it transferred to the storage silo from the data capture point?

c. Audit and clean all the historical data available:
   - Gross and net counts—contactable customers.
   - Time series.
   - Audit of data quality by data field. Identify and quantify all data field gaps.
   - Clean and format data to best practice standards.

d. For databases holding customer data:
   - Identify the data structure and hierarchy.
   - De-dupe and cleaning/formatting processes undertaken.
   - Reporting functionality and establish report sets produced.
   - Data management structure—who is responsible for what.
   - Data flow map tracking data flows into and out of each database and how, if at all, databases are interconnected.
   - As part of this, identify all the data points to which data is transferred to, including any external parties; for example, postal mailing house, e-mail transmission system. Specify how data is sent and at which frequency.

- Data security processes and practices in place.
- Data processing agreements in place conforming to the requirements of Data Protection Laws.
- Presence of any profiling tools. For example, geodemographic or business classification systems.

    e. Define all the user groups: who they are, how do they access data, which data they access, the frequency of access, which data they extract, and how they apply data.

    f. Identify any contractual obligations with suppliers of either equipment, software, or data handling services.

Data Analysis

Initial cut of data analysis of historical data to identify customer dynamics and profiles. The extent of the analyses will be a direct function of the breadth, depth, and quality of the data available. The exercise will cover, for example:

- Build customer segmentation model on dimensions of RFV.
- Source of business by segment by channel by customer.
- Channel/geographical profiles in total and by segment.
- Geodemographic profiles in total and by segment for B2C. Business classification system for B2B.
- Repeat versus new business analysis.
- Attrition rates.
- Engagement levels by type of engagement. For example, e-mail opening/click through rates.
- Promotion analysis of who responds to which type of incentive offer and at which frequency.

CRM Strategy Reference

The CRM strategy, based on these and other inputs as previously described in earlier chapters, used as the reference "bible."

CRM Systems' Solution Requirements

Lay down the CRM System functional specification to enable the CRM strategy to be delivered. This will act as the reference for designing, building, and managing the CRM system's technical solution.

In parallel, appoint a team leader to handle the process to be accountable for the outcome. The position will report to the Board and be the lead principal in all the negotiations. A team of relevant personnel, reporting into this position, to also be appointed with clear relevant skill sets and responsibilities.

The primary inputs will be the current databases/IT operational framework combined with the CRM future requirements of all the departments interfacing with customers (current and potential) embracing marketing, sales, and customer service. The specification will incorporate the following:

a. Laying down the data capture protocol of all the data fields to be captured by each data capture interface where data is gathered. Identify any differences with current/historical protocols and how, if at all, gaps will be filled.

b. Data flow map knitting together all the data movements between data capture sources, data storage, and data processing points. Identify the role(s) and functionality of all parts of the network and how inter-connectivity is envisaged.

c. Lay down data security requirements covering data storage, processing, and transfer to totally comply with all the relevant Data Processing Regulations.

d. Identify all personnel directly involved in servicing the customer covering:
   - Their role(s) interfacing with customers.
   - Their data needs in servicing the customer with the aim of enhancing their customer experience.
   - The information they need to readily and easily impart to the customer.
   - The information they need to gather from the customer.
   - How the data is gathered and to whom is it passed.

This should embrace **all** the contacts with the customer involving, for example, sales personnel's customer contact from telephone conversation to e-mail exchange to meetings to correspondence to draft contracts to signed contracts.

e. Identify all the other users and, for each, specify the following:
   - Their role(s) in data processing, data management, managing customer relationships, selling, data analytics, campaign management, data applications, reporting, and decision making. This will cover all the job positions from Board level down.

   - Their data needs in terms of what information do they require, how do they want to receive the information (channel and format) and how often do they want to receive it.

f. Structure and functionality of the customer centric data warehouse acting as the central data repository for storing and processing all the customer data from all the customer data sources to give a single customer view (see next section).

g. Role and functionality of any Loyalty Apps and how integration should work within the overall system solution.

h. The ongoing data analytics to be undertaken to generate the insights to optimize the commercial return from the CRM strategy. This should specify the data reporting suite to be provided, the data mining tools required, and the statistical techniques to be applied within the analysis framework.

   One cautionary word of advice on the analysis approach. Make data analysis pragmatic and ensure it is not rooted in intellectualism as an academic exercise. It should move away from "analysis paralysis" and provide actionable insights. Data should be de-mystified and those making decisions on the basis of the insights provided should not need to be a data analyst to understand and interpret what the data is telling them.

i. Budget guidelines for design, build, installation, and ongoing support and maintenance.

j. Specification of technical support required if external suppliers are involved in the management and maintenance of any part of the system's solution. Any such supplier should transparently declare any sub-contractor they propose using as part of their solution.

k. Provide a detailed specification of the current customer data operation with the requirement to detail plans to move from the present situation to the recommended solution with timings, actions, and risks. This should highlight data migration as a key component of the plan.

Identify a List of Potential Suppliers and Engage the Briefing Process

Conduct research to identify potential solution providers and draw up a short list.

Specify the briefing process with critical path and methodology involving, for example, face-to-face initial briefing and final proposals presented back with the whole team in attendance for both. Written brief issued and detailed written proposal response.

Lay down criteria for selection adding any criteria to the brief itself.

Commission the briefing process and adopt a formal, structured approach in supplier interfaces.

Decide on CRM technical solution and who to appoint to deliver it. Finalize negotiations, draw up legal agreement, and formalize appointment(s)

The team, under the direction of the team leader, evaluates the proposed CRM technical solutions from a range of solution providers with costs and benefits quantified and assessed against the criteria contained in the brief.

Identify any questions coming out of the evaluation process and return to the relevant solution provider(s) to obtain the answers.

On receipt, the team debates the options and comes to a final view and recommendation.

Recommendation presented to the Board with summary of recommendation circulated beforehand.

Pending Board response, the process continues through to the appointment of external partners with legal service agreement(s) drawn up and signed.

Implementation commences.

Role of Customer Centric Database

The CRM data warehouse has two powerful, highly relevant commercial roles.

Firstly, it is a strategic asset adding value to the worth of the business. Witness Facebook and other online properties where the initial value placed on the business was in relation to the value of its customer base and not its operational profits. The warehouse stores all the customer data with disciplined processes in place to maintain its security, its accuracy, and to keep it up-to-date. It demonstrably boosts the P/E ratio in the valuation of a company.

Secondly, it performs a pivotal role at the center of the CRM technical solution. It is the sole customer data repository holding and processing customer data captured from all data sources including communication to customers on the database and their responses.

As such, it is absolutely vital that deep thought is given to the requirements built into the design functionality but also the operational framework and related working processes.

The factors to consider are listed below:

1. Methods deployed to keep data integrity maintained to exceptional quality standards. Start with a clean database with a program to achieve this. Thereafter, specify the de-dupe process to be used to identify unique customers, with the allocation of a URN attached to each one, address formatting and PAF enhancement. This to include the weighting of variables to match customers—title, first name, surname, address, postcode, e-mail address. (PAF, in the UK postal system, stands for "Postal Address File," which can be used as the reference to verify a customer's address details.)

2. System and process requirements to be compliant with Data Protection Regulations.

3. Data feeds: data exchange points (senders and receivers of data), method, frequency, and identifying one or two way data transfer. Identify any compatibility issues between databases within the network solution with data transfer feasible through API connection or FTP. This should include any connections to Social CRM and Analytical tools. Calculate the time employees currently spend on data management to guide the amount of time released for "thinking and planning" and/or the cost savings if resource is released.

4. Data processing agreement detailing all the processes involved in receiving, storing, extracting, and transferring data internally and externally with security measures consistent with the Data Protection Regulations. This to be to the "best practice" industry standards including the anonymization of data.

5. Database structure and hierarchy linking transactions and customer interactions with the company to individual customers with their profiles attached. Allowance built in for all communications to and from customers to be logged and the status of customer profiles to be updated.

   The customer segment outputs from the customer segmentation model incorporated into the design with the segments dynamically updated from new data entering the database.

6. Facility to add profiling tools. For example, geographic profiling and mapping of the customer universe by drive time/distance from designated point. For example, retail outlet, restaurant, hotel, cinema, and so on. Geodemographic profiling for B2C and business classifications for B2B.

7. Provision of a campaign management tool to enable users to build mailing files and directly export campaign files to mailing house or e-mail transmission engine. File built by either selecting pre-defined segments, previously developed and held on the database, or ad-hoc selections based on a single variable or combination of variables held on the database.

   The functionality to also include the ability to obtain counts from queries and the evaluation of campaign performance via customer response and ROI.

8. Ability to automate communication triggered by specified criteria, contained within the database design, being met, for example, one week after customer has lapsed.

9. Providing users with direct 24/7 access to the database via a front-end application with the ability to, for example:
   • Search and update/amend customer details
   • Access reports
   • Conduct counts
   • Build and execute campaigns

10. Lay down comprehensive specification of reporting requirements via standard reports produced to a fixed frequency (e.g., quarterly) and dynamically updated reports produced in real time and shown through dashboards.

    Reporting on KPIs, other metrics, and evaluations.

    These to be translated into reporting layouts and presentation formats (e.g., Power BI).

11. Identify potential dimensions for future changes in scale. The solution should be scalable with the ability to add new features and modules.

Types of CRM Systems

As a reminder reference.

> The CRM software system is an IT platform for storing all customer data, including financial and communication interactions with the company, generated across multiple channels. It consolidates and enters customer information into a single CRM database so business users can more easily access and manage it.

There are two core routes to access CRM technology:

On-Premise CRM

A system essentially purchased off the shelf and tailored to a company's needs to whatever degree is feasible within the system design itself. The software sits on the company's own servers. Therefore, all the aspects of

IT management resides with the company—administration, control, security, and maintenance of the database and company information. The company purchases usage licenses upfront for the system from the CRM software vendor and assumes the cost of any upgrades.

The software is installed on the desktop computers for all the users.

The migration of the data into the software environment is the responsibility of the company and usually requires a prolonged installation process to fully integrate a company's data.

Cloud Based CRM

A web based application, hosted by external parties, with data and programs residing on their global network of secure data centers instead of on the company's hard drive as in the on-premise route. As such, there is typically no software to be downloaded and installed on each individual user's computer with the CRM system sitting entirely online with the company effectively renting the service.

SaaS (Software as a Service) is the most common type of cloud computing, delivering complete, user-ready applications over the Internet. Sometimes referred to as "On demand CRM."

Data is stored on an external, remote network that employees can access anytime, anywhere there is an internet connection. Clients upload their customer data to the host's servers and interact with the data using their web browsers.

Effectively, cloud computing is a kind of outsourcing of software, data storage, and processing. Users access applications and files by logging in from any device that has an internet connection. In this context, there are some powerful reasons for it to be considered: processing power is freed up, sharing and collaboration is facilitated, and it allows secure mobile access regardless of where the user is or what device is being used.

In summary, cloud computing is marketed as a more efficient way of delivering CRM computing solutions. Payment to the service provider for software and service environments is subscription based with users paying a monthly fee instead of buying licenses. The software and platforms are managed by the providers and are updated continuously for maximum performance and security.

Computing power is lodged in a bank of external servers, so users can tap into extra capacity if required either to handle short term spikes or long-term functionality expansion. Multiple users in a company can access shared programs or files and collaborate in real time from different locations.

There are two basic approaches: a bespoke solution or a proprietary system sourced via one of the major vendors such as Salesforce, Microsoft, SAP, and Oracle.

The concept and thinking behind a bespoke solution is identical to the proprietary system with data stored remotely in the "cloud" in an external network with users directly accessing via any device (PC, laptop, tablet, smartphone) by an internet connection. The only difference is that, as the name suggests, the bespoke solution is tailored specifically to the client's requirements.

A conceptual design of a bespoke solution is shown below in Figure 7.3 based on a system for a hotel. Compatible with this, the database structure is depicted in Figure 7.4, which acts as the engine room for data management and processing with one key feature being campaign planning as shown in Figure 7.5.

Some of the top-line differences between bespoke and proprietary systems are summarized below in Table 7.1:

Depending on their CRM specification and selection criteria, Companies should initially conduct a broad sweep of options (On-premise, SaaS, Bespoke CRM, and Open Source CRM) before narrowing it down to those offering the closest fit and focusing on suppliers within them.

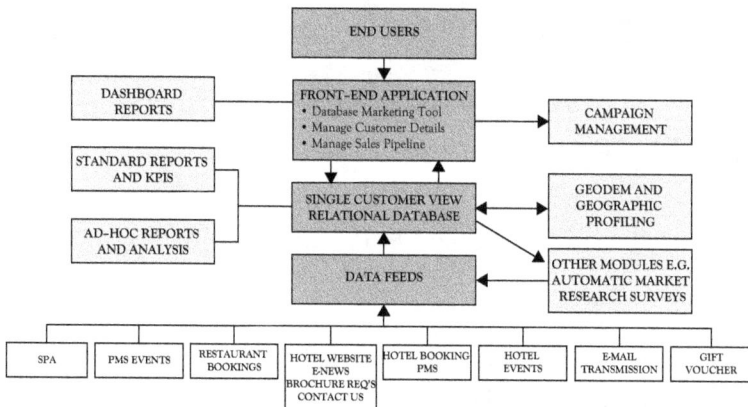

Figure 7.3 **CRM database solution based on a hotel model**

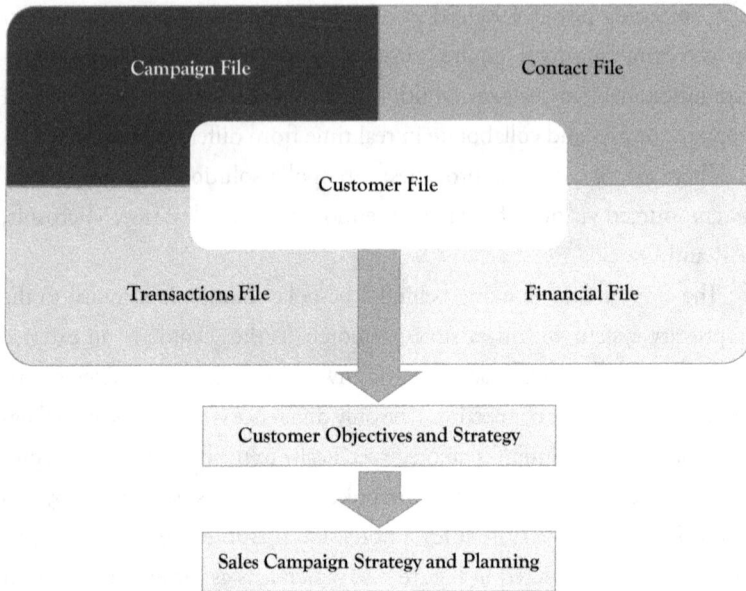

Figure 7.4 Database structure

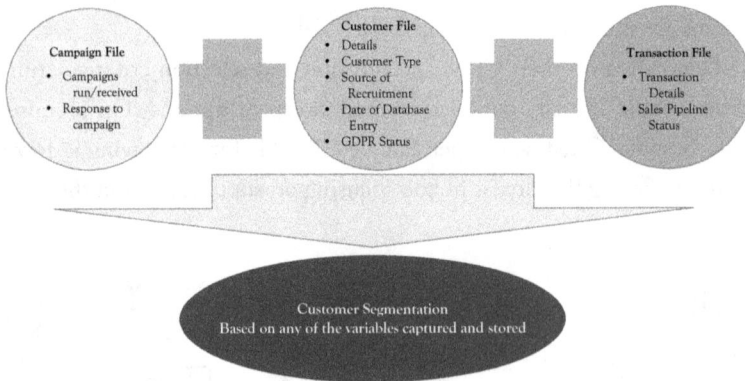

Figure 7.5 Campaign planning

Pros and Cons of SaaS Versus On-Premise

Cons

- Data security. The company does not itself physically control the storage and maintenance of the data. It is stored in the "cloud" under the management of a third party and the serv-

Table 7.1 Bespoke solutions versus Proprietary solutions

	BESPOKE	PROPRIETARY
1.	Bespoke is designed to meet client's CRM specification. Totally tailored to client needs in all the aspects of functionality including, for example, the following more easily addressed: • Customizable persona • Additional geodemographics • Additional geocoding for mapping and distance • Data matching and SCV via de-dupe software	Client fits design and functionality of the proprietary system but "One size does not necessarily fit all." Important to check the customizable fields the generic product under consideration has and whether it gives you the tailored information you need when you want it.
2.	Bespoke designed to be scalable to accommodate growth in a financially structured way. Client initially pays for what they need with functionality added easily as requirements evolve, such as extra modules.	Proprietary system's functional spec can often be "over spec" with the client paying for functionality not required. Extra capacity is not the issue—more to do with expanding the functionality.
3.	A client system needs to have the in-built flexibility to be able to evolve in line with usage.	The cost of amending a proprietary system to meet the changing specific needs of an individual client can be excessive.
4.	A bespoke system/solution provider can be more "fleet of foot" and responsive to client requests for functional changes.	A client can be required to wait for development roadmaps for their functional change requirements.
5.	The technical and operational support provided by a bespoke solutions provider can be more responsive through telephone support, ops manuals, and onsite training.	Ongoing technical and operational support of a proprietary supplier can often be slow in comparison with delays linked to the account management structure and volume of traffic.
6.	A bespoke system solution provider can have the skill set to advise on the application of data with a major input on the development of the CRM strategy.	A proprietary system solution provider primarily solely specializes in the software and do not, in the main, have CRM consultancy services; albeit they have a number of case studies.
7.	By definition, bespoke solutions are not based on existing software; albeit some of the coding will be common to all client solutions. As such, the software design solution cannot be demonstrated; albeit features from other systems built can be.	Proprietary systems use existing, generic software available to all the existing and potential clients. Hence, case studies can be gone through and the software readily demonstrated enabling the client to see what they will be buying.
8.	Solution providers are smaller in size with related less back-up resources.	Vendors are of a large size and scale providing higher confidence levels.

Note: There is an Open Source CRM system alternative to SaaS; where source code is made available for companies to make alterations at no cost to the company employing the system. Open Source CRM systems also enable the addition and customization of data links on social media channels assisting companies to improve social CRM practices. Examples of Open Source Platforms are Oro CRM, Suite CRM, and Sugar CRM.

ers may be located in geographical areas outside, for example, the UK with related Data Protection ramifications. On both counts, it is of paramount importance that a legally binding Data Processing Agreement is in place if this route is pursued.

- There may be compatibility issues when data is initially migrated from a company's internal system to the cloud. Complications can arise when moving data to the cloud and working with disparate systems. Often, in the world of IT, things invariably sound easy but prove difficult in practice.

- Paying subscription fees can be more costly than on premise models over time.

- Unexpected costs can arise as the business grows and needs to evolve. Nine times out of ten, this can happen when the users start using the system and get the "touchy feely" experience and find, in practice, the system's deficiencies and strengths.

- The company relies on the hosting provider for any updates and the timing of updates. This can prove to be a frustrating and costly experience.

- Once commissioned and in use, the system's rigidity and functionality can turn out to be a negative. Not necessarily because of the system itself, but because either the company has made a "bum" decision or has not properly got everybody on board beforehand and then trained them properly.

Pros

- No need to go through time consuming and complex installation and implementation processes in locating software on all desktop computers. No hardware to install at the start or maintain thereafter.

- No significant up front Capex on IT infrastructure or data center costs.

- Updates and repairs done by the hosting provider with automatic software updates. The cloud system is updated in real time by the hosting provider with no system downtime or additional charges due to hardware issues.

- The company's IT department's service and maintenance responsibilities are scaled down.
- The infrastructure can grow with the company as its business expands. This relates to the storage and processing capacity and not necessarily the software database structure.
- Offsite storage of company (and client data where relevant) makes it less vulnerable to onsite disasters.
- The entire company's team can quickly view, access, and share the same customer data in real time across different channels anytime from anywhere on any device.

Other CRM Tools

The systems outlined are best described as "Operational CRM" to which other CRM "tools" can be added to increase the capability of the overall system, such as:

a. Analytical CRM uses data mining and pattern recognition to provide the more in-depth and sensitive insights to better understand market trends and customers' wants and needs. The enriched knowledge can add value to each stage of the customer journey from lead generation to customer retention, but is particularly helpful in understanding how to deliver genuine customer satisfaction.

b. Collaborative CRM where data is pooled among data partners. This is relevant to companies where they have several product/service divisions who are marketing to a common, overlapping universe. For example, in the UK, Kingfisher plc through its two retail operations of B & Q and Screwfix. Obviously, any such activity has to be totally compliant to the Data Protection Regulations, which means, up front, the customer needs to understand what they are signing up to.

c. S-CRM (Social Customer Relationship Management).** Information integration requires the assimilation of customer information from all touch points: from different data sources to create a coherent picture of customers, to develop a single customer view, and collect information about their interaction with the company.

In this context, social media is progressively escalating in importance as a primary data source.

However, there are some fundamental differences with this channel compared to the others:

- In the traditional CRM approach, data is logged by a third party, usually with some time gap after the event has occurred. The S-CRM approach incorporates real time data for real time information with data generated directly by customers. With every engagement with customers on social media, more data is created.
- The focus of CRM has traditionally consisted of one-way communication between company and customer. An S-CRM system assumes continuous exchange of experiences; not only between company and customer but also between individual customers.
- Most data captured through social media is unstructured with most dialogue being open text. Therefore, for such data to be useful, it needs to be transformed by data or text mining (TM) before it can be integrated with CRM systems.

Social media presents an Open Forum for customers to engage in a dialogue among themselves to share their experiences with a company; whether they are airing grievances or promoting products. Companies must be interested in capturing such customer sentiments to elicit the likelihood of recommending products and their overall satisfaction—good or bad. Plugging into customer communities where customers post reviews of products and can engage with other customers to troubleshoot issues or research products in real time is also beneficial. Communities can provide low level customer service for certain kinds of problems and reduce the number of contact center calls. They can also provide new product ideas or feedback that companies can use in lieu of feedback from Market Research Groups.

To add value to customer interactions on social media, companies can access various S-CRM tools that monitor social media conversations; from specific mentions of a company or its brands to the frequency of keywords used. This can help to determine their target audience related to the platforms they use. Also to analyze social media feedback and address customer queries and issues.

In summary, S-CRM enables companies to interact directly with their customers in real time using a variety of social media platforms. Social media technologies have the capability to bring customers and companies closer together through two-way interactions and dialogue. The S-CRM system supports customer information management, and therefore, helps improve dialogue with customers by accessing data from the new channels of communication. This is critical to many companies where customers are active in the social media environment because it is the catalyst to new ways of behaving with community members sharing experiences and views but, above all, many of which are rooted in emotions. Some of these can be highly damaging and, reflective of the medium, can spread like a prairie fire.

The following quotes reinforce the growing importance of S-CRM:

- "The business potential of unstructured external social media is very high, considering that 80% of the world's data is unstructured and it is growing at 15 times the rate of structured data." (Pritchard, 2012)
- "As the world is growing digital day by day, consumers' behaviour is also changing rapidly due to technological intervention in their day-to-day life. In this period, CRM is continuously developing as one of the most beneficial business tools to satisfy customers and provide them with the values that they require most." (Rai, 2014)
- "S-CRM does not nullify the efforts developed by CRM marketing but provides a supplement, reinforcing the company's customer focus and facilitating knowledge of behaviours, attitudes and feelings." (Woodcock, Green, and Stacey, 2011)

**(F.A. Buttle, Customer relationship management: concept and tools, ResearchGate, accessed April 17, 2019), (Fraser, Helms, and Spruit 2011), (Greenberg 2010), (Jelonek n.d.), (Pritchard 2012), (Rouse, Ehrens, and Kiwak, CRM – customer relationship management, WhatIs.

com, accessed April 23, 2019), (Santos, Almeida, and Monteiro 2013), (Scullin, Fjermestad, and Romano 2004)

One further major technology development which will generally impact CRM is "artificial Intelligence" (AI).***

The goal of improving the customer experience, and thereby customer satisfaction, is a leading candidate for investments in artificial intelligence, which can help enhance personalized experiences by recognizing customers, knowing them, and then anticipating their needs. AI analyses, classifies, and predicts data faster, in greater volume, and more extensively than humans without AI. For example, in S-CRM, it will enhance understanding through conversational interfaces and augmented analytics. Natural Language Processing (NLP) is used to analyze word choice to provide a deeper level of psychological insight with the model continuously improved by learning from conversations it has with people.

AI's application will improve predictions by spotting trends buried in data, underpin more accurate decisions, and help to understand how customers interpret issues and make decisions that will potentially be very powerful in improving the customer experience.

Gartner predicts that by 2021, 15% of all customer service interactions will be completely handled by AI, an increase of 400% from 2017.
(Olive Huang, Research Vice-President, Gartner, gartner.com, accessed July 28, 2020)

While its adoption is still early, it is easy to see how the potential impact of AI can be transformational.

***(Melissa Davis, How to use AI to improve the customer experience, Gartner, accessed April 11, 2018)

Benefits of Cloud Based System

There are a number of generic benefits from using SaaS with their relevance and commercial impact varying according to each company's circumstances.

A summary of the major benefits are listed below:

a. Financial modeling can be undertaken with, in the short term, a high degree of certainty. The following factors can be identified:

- Cloud based systems are priced on the number of users and the features required. Hence, the variable cost of usage can be quantified and, in so doing, add in any impact on cost from the volume of data and backup requirements.

- Front-end costs in terms of any capital outlay and setting up—installation and implementation covering data migration, training, and so on. The cloud computing solution depresses the need for large capital investments in infrastructure and software.

- Operational running costs. Savings need to be accounted for including, for example:

  ○ Reduced in-house IT support

  ○ No need for employees to manually back up data

  ○ Employees no longer tethered to the office with more productive use of time

  ○ Eliminates need to update software every few years to buy the latest version of important programs

  ○ Erases need for duplicate versions of documents stored on multiple devices with changes made by pinging e-mail files back and forth

  ○ Fast on-demand data delivery

This exercise is essential because moving to a cloud solution effectively shifts costs from a capital budget to an operating budget focus.

Hence, a capital and operational cost model can be built and compared to a company's current model and alternative solutions. In this context, the cost/benefit balance equation is: reduced up-front costs + predictable system usage pricing in the short term if no change in requirements + less system downtime or additional charges due to server maintenance/upgrading because cloud system is updated in real time by the service provider + reduced company departmental IT costs + other departmental operational cost savings = Cloud computing subscription costs + set up costs.

b. Increased collaboration and shared information generates higher levels of productivity and management effectiveness. Shared platforms make working together simpler with common tools, common data definitions, formats, and reporting. Information is available to anyone who needs it at anytime from anywhere.

c. Cloud computing has the flexibility to scale up or down as needed. The following can be added or contracted: bandwidth, number of users, services, and number of cloud service providers. Large capital investments in infrastructure is not a shoo-in to accommodate growth. But, the architecture should be reviewed periodically to make sure the system is working efficiently. However, fundamentally, you should have made sure at the outset of the scope of the system's functionality and the cost, timing and feasibility of making any adjustments and, most importantly, identify the limitations and the no-go areas for adding to the functionality.

d. Data security. In essence, any computer connected to the Internet or a network is potentially vulnerable to outside threat.

Although no system is completely fool proof, Cloud service providers are generally much better at protecting data than their in-house counterparts for two main reasons:

- They have large resources with large spend on deeply embedded security measures that far exceeds that of most other enterprises. They have robust processes in place to ensure data is protected. Information is encrypted and backed up continuously with systems monitored for any security vulnerabilities. Top vendors invest to stay "ahead of the curve," employing experts in computer science and cybersecurity to keep systems updated with the latest encryption technology.
Many cloud providers automatically create backups using the latest hardware and software to operate systems in a way that smaller companies cannot. This has the additional benefit of

optimizing reliability in minimizing, if not eliminating, any downtime.

- SaaS providers are also helped by the complexity of their operations, which adds a further layer of security. Cyber criminals need to find and gain access to the right data center to compromise a company's data even if they know the company's Cloud provider because data can be located in multi-sites and/or on shared storage space.

Service Level Agreement (SLA)

An SLA is the main contract between a company and the cloud service provider that serves as the blueprint of the services to be supplied and a warranty against the delivery of such services. It is an all-embracing agreement covering everything from security measures and data handling to service interruptions and data breaches.

This is a legal document and should be appropriately crafted and scrutinized to the nth degree to ensure that all the service specifications are covered and clearly written in an unequivocal manner leaving no scope for interpretation with zero "wriggle" room.

The SLA should spell out the following:

a. System delivery performance measures covering, for example:
  - Uptime %.
  - Dealing with a catastrophic event with clear definitions of such events. This to include "force majeure" classified events.
  - Back up servers and procedures to ensure there are no service disruptions.
  - Continuous performance monitoring methodology including reporting.
  - Quantify all relevant performance metrics. Indicators could include capacity (number of users who can access the cloud at any given point in time) and response time for processing customer interactions.
  - Refund policy and mechanism in the event of SLA metrics not being met.

- What log information will be provided and will it be in a format that, for example, can be imported into operational analysis software.

b. Support to help get the most out of the system as well as help when something goes wrong. For example:
   - Testing regime before committing.
   - Scope, cost, and flexibility of support options: skilled trained professional to deal with, knowledge base to self-help. For example, video tutorials, FAQs, forums, operating manuals, online help (time when available), direct telephone support (time when available and response time), onsite training, off site seminars.

c. Where data is located?

d. Who owns the data?

e. What data controls are in place?

f. How data is protected in transit?

g. How data is protected once it is in the cloud?

h. Aspects of security. Ensure data is held and managed to be fully compliant with the Data Protection Regulations and other industry regulations, only available to those authorized to access it, guaranteed never to be shared or sold to third parties.

i. Operationally, confirm parameters underwriting the definition of data being "readily available as and when you need it" and the specification of formats for data downloads.

j. Who in the cloud service provider's organization has access to different types/levels of data?

k. What password policies and authorization processes will be used?

l. Is a Data Processing Agreement in place, which can form part of the SLA?

m. Spell out the consequences and penalties of any condition contained in the SLA being broken.

n. Address exit planning and the conditions controlling exit.

o. Business review procedures.

Some Practicalities

We have heard the expression "it takes two to tango." Well, it equally applies here.

Listed below is an outline practical checklist to help guide the selection process and decision making from the company's side:

a. Always remember one of the main CRM challenges. Without proper management, a CRM system can become little more than a glorified database in which customer information is stored; irrespective of the advancement in CRM technology. At the top level, make sure there is a cast iron CRM strategy in place to which everyone "lock stock and barrel" are signed up to and on board with. At the next level, make sure data sets will be fully connected, distributed, and organized so that users can easily access the information they need. Remember, you can only achieve a Single Customer View if data sets are connected and organized to deliver that perspective. In this context, check and confirm data connectivity through APIs.

b. We all know the expression "rubbish in, rubbish out." This is certainly apt for data, and all your efforts will be wasted unless, from the outset, you solemnly commit to undertake the following:
   - Identify the data you want and update and unify your data capture protocols accordingly across all the data capture points.
   - Clean existing customer data to eliminate duplicates and incomplete records (or find ways of completing them) and outdated information. This is an essential task before supplementing with new and external sources of data.
   - Enhance name, address, postcode, and formatting.

c. Ensure all the users have been exposed to and agree the usability of the system. It needs to be user friendly and there needs to be a cohesive plan to get users up to speed as quickly and effectively as possible. Check on whether you can test the application and whether there is a free trial you can engage to check how intuitive the interface is?

   d. Check contractual options prior to negotiations. Areas to consider:
- Flexibility in scaling up cloud services and capacity as and when you need them
- Monthly or annual subscription and the amount of any capital investment involved, if at all
- Discount offers for longer-term commitments
- Degree to which there are easy protective steps to cancel the service

   e. Check whether your data will be kept on a communal database (multi-tenancy) with your data tagged to separate it from the others or on its own database (single tenancy) and software.

      The choice will be a trade-off between service requirements (data volume, bandwidth required, and system functionality complexity), scalability, security, reliability, customization, and cost.

   f. Check out credentials of potential vendors; how long in business, their reputation in the market place, client references, development plans to accommodate technological changes.

   g. Specify all the external third parties involved in capturing data related to the customers. These will obviously vary by industry sector but, for example, could include ticketing agencies, table booking sites for restaurants, delivery agents, Wi-Fi check-ins, social media connections, online ordering, and so on. Audit and validate their ability to provide access to your customer records. These parties do not always allow for API access or the data can simply not be shared due to either contractual arrangements or doing so will contravene the Data Protection regulations.

Practical Advice from an IT Perspective

CRM is a wide ranging subject with different management functions involved with varying skill sets. In this context, given the specialist nature of CRM technology, I thought it beneficial to elicit the views from senior managers with extensive corporate experience heading IT functions, to give their technical advice on how to best approach a CRM system solution to deliver a successful result. To view this on two dimensions. Firstly, the conditions that must be in place for the CRM system to fulfill its potential. Secondly, the steps to follow to plan, install, and apply the CRM system to ensure its success.

It is intended to provide a practical guide and technical insight to complement my own views and observations, thereby giving the reader a full picture of how to approach this important spoke in the CRM wheel.

I feature one view below, which reflects the collective views of those consulted.

Viewpoint from Rene Hoondert

Background

Rene is a commercially focused Information System Director with 25 years' experience in Information Technology, with a degree in Business Economics. He has implemented global CRM solutions in the consumer goods industry and is experienced in driving the delivery of complex business transformation programs in demanding environments. He has an excellent record of working closely with board-level stakeholders in an international environment to define IS strategies and translate them into successful delivery.

CRM Implementation Strategy

The implementation of a CRM system solution can play a pivotal role, as part of a CRM strategy, in transforming a company's commercial performance onto a higher plane. If the power of a CRM system is fully harnessed, it can have a significant impact on a company's business performance, on customer revenue development, and cost efficiency. However, in practice, many CRM projects fail, and as a result, companies do not realize the prize due to a number of different reasons.

There are a number of conditions that must be in place for the CRM system to fulfill its potential:

1. The CRM system should always be a part of a wider CRM business strategy and not treated as a technology installation project as such. For CRM to succeed in a company, the Sales and Marketing teams need to develop an overarching CRM business strat-

egy, before deciding on the CRM technology design/selection and before implementing a CRM technology platform.

2. The CRM business strategy needs to be owned by the Board of Directors, with the customer at its center with the singular objective to optimize revenues and profit through focusing on customer development, increasing their loyalty and ratcheting up the efficiency in processes whilst enhancing the customer experience. It is "top down" and embraces and impacts:

- The company structure
- Its organization
- Its systems, data, and processes
- Its culture and ethos
- Training and fully supporting all personnel, particularly those who are customer interfacing, to ensure they are properly equipped to fulfill their responsibilities

3. There needs to be an acknowledgment that implementing a CRM strategy with an underlying CRM technology platform is not trivial and is more of a journey than some quick fix solution. In order to gain real competitive advantage through CRM, the CRM strategy needs to be sound and the CRM technology solution needs to be sophisticated. The Board of Directors will have to be prepared to sign-up to a CRM journey, during which, the CRM strategy will evolve and improve over time. The CRM system implementation should be phased, with clearly defined costs and deliverables for the first and most essential phases.

4. After each phase of delivery of the CRM systems solution, a formal post-implementation review is required to determine the extent to which the system is meeting the business requirements and is actually driving customer excellence and profit optimization. The company needs to be prepared to learn and adjust when CRM system's usage in day-to-day reality proves different than what was anticipated during the design at the drawing board. This could mean re-engineering certain parts of the CRM philosophy or rewriting parts of the system's specifications, in order to make the solution fit for purpose and better tailored to business practices.

5. An essential condition for a successful implementation is to have a proper implementation team in place to deliver the solution. The implementation team should include a combination of the following people:
   - The people who developed the wider CRM business strategy
   - IS (Information Systems) staff
   - CRM Process Owners
   - Future key users of the system
   - Managers and analysts who will be using the CRM data

   Dependent on the level of complexity and the required sophistication of the CRM system, the Board of Directors needs to be prepared to put an implementation team in place with a number of full-time staff, who are specifically incentivized to make the implementation project a success.

6. Think big but start small. Breakdown the project into manageable pieces and deliver tangible results after every project phase, to ensure stakeholders can see the value of the solution, and to ensure project team members remain motivated and will continue to recognize the potential of the future solution.

7. Establish a strong governance structure to control the implementation project and keep everyone onboard. Senior executives of the IS function and the Sales and Marketing functions need to co-own the project and feel equally responsible for delivering the business case.

8. Identify and design the required interfaces of the CRM system with other information systems, such as Financial Accounting systems, Marketing Databases, or reporting solutions.

9. Strike the right balance between the deployment of company internal resources and outside contractors and hired consultants. Implementing a CRM system is not like buying a new piece of machinery to run with for the next 10+ years! CRM implementations are complex and because business processes within a company are unique, there's never a straight copy and paste scenario from another implementation. Internal resources have more knowledge and need to own the process changes. External staff bring in new perspectives and have specific knowledge of the systems and tools. Over-reliance on external staff

makes project deadlines slip, results in lack of internal ownership, and risks losing the focus on the original project objectives. Over-reliance on internal staff could lack innovation and risks doing the same thing all over again.

10. Prepare a Business Intelligence strategy alongside the CRM implementation strategy. Typically, at the start of a CRM implementation project, the focus is still very much on the new CRM processes and the new ways of working, such as screen navigation, process design, and populating the system with the right insights to make it user-friendly. As the CRM system matures and data is streaming-in on a daily basis, the focus of the CRM implementation project changes to aggregating and reporting the data in an efficient way. The challenge that then comes up is on how to combine the new CRM data with data that is already available from other systems in the company and data from alternative (external) sources.

Steps Involved in Implementing a CRM Solution

1. Develop a system requirements specification, including the following elements:
   a. Summary of the CRM vision statement.
   b. Summary of the Corporate IS vision and where CRM fits into the overall systems' landscape.
   c. Description of current business processes and ways of working.
   d. Description of the different user groups and their specific roles in the processes.
   e. Identify all personnel involved in servicing the customer, their roles, their data/processing needs, their training requirements, and so on.
   f. Identify links and dependencies of the new CRM processes and CRM data to external organizations; such as supply chain partners, logistics service providers, marketing agencies to input data, and so on
   g. Describe the limitations in the current ways of working and clearly articulate the changes required.
   h. Describe the status of current data held.

  i. Identify all the current data capture points, data fields captured, how captured, where stored, and so on.

  j. Reporting and analysis requirements, including a description of the contribution of the CRM system to the Business Intelligence strategy and/or Company Data Warehouse(s).

  k. Describe the requirements for data mining tools and statistical techniques.

  l. Data integration requirements (interfaces to other systems).

  m. Data security requirements.

2. Audit and clean historical data

  a. Conduct a full audit of all databases holding customer data with data structure, reporting functionality, data management structure, data security processes and practices, and so on.

  b. Define all the user groups and how data is applied.

  c. Identify any contractual obligations with all the external parties involved in the data.

  d. Data analysis. Initial cut of historical data to identify customer dynamics and profiles. Build customer segmentation model on dimensions of RFV and so on.

3. Scoping out a customer segmentation strategy based on the above and other relevant inputs.

4. Setup a project implementation team, including a project team leader from the IS side and a project team leader from the business side (typically from Sales or Marketing). The IS project leader is accountable for delivering the systems solution; the Business project leader is accountable for delivering the new processes and new ways of working.

5. Specify the post-implementation support organization and future needs to run the new CRM solution, both from an IS technical support perspective and from a business perspective (data administrators, field sale trainers, reporting analysts etc.).

6. Specify where the data will be held and how security will be ensured, including data protection and disaster recovery plans.

7. Setup a project budget to design, build, and install the new system, including ongoing running costs for support and maintenance.

8. Prepare a high-level Business Case for the project and present this to the Board of Directors, informing them about the implementa-

tion costs, the deliverables, the project milestones, and the payback for this kind of investment. Board approval of the Business Case is required before taking the next steps of in-depth engagement with software vendors and solution delivery partners.

9. Identify a list of potential suppliers of CRM software and engage the briefing process.

10. Identify a list of potential suppliers of CRM solution delivery partners and engage the briefing process.

11. Document 1 or more "Request(s) for Proposal (RFP)" and submit this to a selection of software vendors and solution delivery partners, asking them to prepare a written response and a legally binding quotation.

12. Schedule vendor presentations of the solutions on offer and how to deliver these solutions. Broad participation from different departments within the company is required to ensure stakeholder buy-in.

13. Decide on CRM technical solution and who to appoint to deliver it. Engage procurement practices for the software, the hardware and the data centers, finalize the negotiations, draw up the legal agreements.

14. Update the Business Case, incorporating all financial information from the RFP and the legally binding quotes of the selected software provider and the selected solution delivery partner.

15. Submit an Investment Application to the Board of Directors to secure the funding and the implementation resources.

16. Formalize the appointment(s) of external suppliers.

17. Document the CRM implementation project plan and breakdown the different phases of the implementation methodology.

18. Establish a plan for change management and document the training plan for different user groups.

19. Setup the Governance Process and define control points within the governance framework.

20. Appoint the project implementation team and kick-off the implementation!

*(act.com, What is CRM? accessed March 5, 2020), (Dr. G. Babu, 2016), (Baran, Zerres, and Zerres, Customer Relationship Management, Bookboon.com, accessed May 30, 2019), (Cambra-Fierro, Centeno,

Olavarria, and Vazquez – Carrasco, 2017), (DHL Masterclass.com, accessed December 15, 2019), (Innovation PEI – Province of Ontario, Customer Relationship Management, accessed May 15, 2019), (Jennifer Lund, What is CRM? The Definitive Guide to Success, Superoffice. com, accessed April 23, 2019), (Parvatiyar and Sheth 2002), (Rai 2014), (Rouse, Ehrens, and Kiwak, CRM – customer relationship management, WhatIs.com, accessed April 23, 2019), (Salesforce.com, What is CRM?, accessed April 23, 2019), (Wikipedia, s.v.v. Customer –relationship management, accessed April 23, 2019, https://en.wikipedia.org/wiki/customer-relationship-management)

Some Key Thoughts to Reflect on if You Are Considering/Reviewing CRM

The CRM system solution is the engine room of the CRM car. To continue the analogy, it can help you engage top gear to accelerate your revenue and profit whilst improving the engine's cost efficiency in running the business operations. The commercial prize on offer is enormous. But, first of all, you need to design the car (the CRM strategy) and then the engine best suited to drive it (the CRM system solution).

It is therefore imperative that you get it right!

It is a complex and multi-layered subject. The chapter reflects this by comprehensively delving into all the angles, issues and factors to consider to design and implement a successful CRM solution with the mission of "leaving no stone unturned."

CRM involves significant financial investment and it is essential it is addressed in the most disciplined and detailed manner to ensure you select the optimum solution and one that delivers the commercial payback on the investment. The chapter fulfills the role of being a pragmatic but sound guide and, given the gravity and impact of CRM systems on the overall business performance, I encourage you to read and absorb it from beginning to end.

All aspects of CRM systems are important and link together. You should follow the sections in a sequential order whilst, at each stage, pausing to assess how your business measures up against the reference provided and where, if at all, you need to revisit and re-address your approach. The sections, in order, are:

1. An overview of what CRM systems are and their role(s) in delivering the CRM strategy.

2. Features of CRM systems divided into functions and applications. A useful check list.

3. CRM system benefits. If you have a CRM system already in place, use as a reference to check whether you are deriving all the commercial benefits available by fully and properly applying a CRM system solution. If you are considering a CRM system, use it as an input into drawing up your functional specification and for your commercial appraisal.

4. The CRM system solution specification. This is your template to draw up your specification as the reference for defining and selecting the solution. This, arguably, is the most important section in the chapter. In reality, it is difficult to decide on a solution unless you have, in the first instance, defined what you want!

5. Role of the customer centric database. Get this right and you are half way there!

6. Types of CRM systems. This section explores the technical nuances of the different CRM technologies and CRM tools available with the roles and pros and cons of each outlined and defined.

7. Benefits of a Cloud based system. This details the generic benefits from using SaaS with their relevance and commercial impact varying according to your company's circumstances.

8. Service Level Agreements (SLA). This provides a guide on drawing up an SLA once you are in a position to place a contract with your CRM software provider. Once again, it is an imperative to tick all the legal boxes to ensure both parties understand their responsibilities and perform accordingly within a legal framework.

9. This section outlines the areas you need to cover from your internal perspective.

10. Views expressed by a senior Information Technology Director who has been responsible for delivering CRM system solutions for his companies. He provides a practical slant on what needs to be done to give the best chance of success in selecting and operating a CRM system solution and, as such, gives a really useful cross reference guide.

Finally, to hammer the nail in, I talked at length with a friend of mine, Dick Snow, who has recently retired following a career in IT with a general focus on CRM and particular specialization in customer service and contact centers. He project managed several implementations of Oracle's CRM system and Clarify, whilst also acting as the partner manager with "salesforce" on joint strategies and implementations on behalf of companies he worked for.

He tabled 7 "golden nuggets," which I pass onto you as the last of the practical guides for you to refer to and apply:

7 commandments according to Dick

1. **Recognize the importance of the R factor**

   One of his first memories was a talk given by a psychiatrist to one of the founding CRM software vendors. The theme of the talk was that all relationships (husband/wife, partners, companies/customers, etc.) are founded on a series of interactions; some good, some not so good —the more that are good, the better the relationship. Organizations interact with potential and existing customers through many channels and involve every part of the organization. Get every interaction right and the relationship will be good; get too many wrong and the customer is likely to stop buying from the company and possibly post less than positive comments on social media. So, to get the "R" back into CRM requires optimizing every single interaction.

2. **CRM is bigger than the technology**

   CRM should therefore never be thought of as just a technology solution. CRM is as much, if not more so, about process and human resources as it is about technology. Organizations must therefore determine how any system can support enterprise processes and the staff interfacing with customers; in particular, how customers move between marketing, sales, service, and finance.

3. **Engage all parties**

   To achieve this, organizations must involve all the relevant functions throughout the whole process of selecting and installing a system, from defining requirements through product selection, implementation, and acceptance including external partners such as contact centers and web site teams.

4. **Walk before you run**

Do not over specify the functional requirements at the beginning. Get the core CRM functionality right and ensure the vendors can support them with either standard capabilities or customizations.

5. **Data is the Holy Grail**

Customer data is managed in ALL departments so it must be right—accurate, timely, and to common definitions. This must enable all the customer facing staff, including contact centers, to have direct access to customer data with the ability to modify and add to customer data.

6. **Integration is sacrosanct**

A CRM system does not stand alone and must integrate with and share data with other systems. Any implementation plan should therefore pay attention to how the CRM system will integrate with and share data with all the relevant systems.

7. **Agents of change**

The overall objective of any CRM program should be:

- Increase customer acquisition through more focused marketing and sales.
- Increase customer value by increasing purchasing, reducing support costs, and improving customer retention.

Acceptance of the software should therefore be undertaken as a component of an enterprise wide change program. It is an absolute imperative that companies make the required people and process changes to extract full value from their selected CRM system and meet their strategic CRM objectives. It's amazing the number of companies that "pay lip service" and fail to engage the change in culture, people, and process required to make it work and are confused when it doesn't!

CHAPTER 8

B2B

Introduction

All the CRM principles and practices apply to B2B, but even more so with a degree of escalation in the importance of managing the sales process for two primary reasons:

- Customers have all the transaction invoices linked to them to give a complete sales history.
- The company is dealing directly with the primary customer who is purchasing the product or service.

We can place this in the context of the CRM framework.

At the topline, CRM is a strategic approach to the management of a company's interaction with current and potential customers.

The CRM software system is the primary tool that enables a company to accomplish this with contact management, sales management, and more. It facilitates an organization's relationship with individual customers throughout their lifecycle from finding and recruiting new customers, winning new business, and prioritizing support and additional services throughout the relationship with them.

The important dimension in B2B is to identify and break down the customer facing processes to define their roles and contribution to customer management.

Customer Facing Processes

The CRM strategy focus is on the customer facing processes and makes them better in terms of meeting customer needs. These can be segregated into their key component parts as below:

Marketing

- Customer segmentation
- Campaign development
- Campaign execution
- Campaign evaluation
- Project/event management
- Customer profitability with finance

Sales

- Lead management
- Account management
- Pipeline management
- Cross-selling and up-selling
- Activity management
- Customer development and retention
- Confronting and solving issues in a timely and proactive manner

Customer Service

- Request management
- Service tracking
- Complaints management
- Prioritization
- SLA agreements
- Account enquiries
- Status reports
- Monitoring/reporting on key KPIs. For example, time taken to answer a call
- Order status

In B2B, unlike B2C, the sales function has the primary role in articulating the product/service benefits, converting the initial sale, and developing customers thereafter by directly interfacing with them. In B2C, in contrast, as earlier discussed, there is the juxtaposition between the ultimate consumer of the product/service and the customer through which you reach the ultimate consumer and, in many market sectors, they are not one and the same. The marketing function has the primary role for managing the consumer interface, whereas the sales function has the primary role for managing the customer interface.

In this context, the key factors to take on board to extract the maximum CRM benefits from the sales and customer service processes are:

A. The target audience

The target audience, from a sales perspective, needs to be defined on two levels. Firstly, allocating the company to a business classification. In this way, the company can know the universe of the classification, through external research, and therefore, can measure the penetration of the universe achieved and the remaining potential.

Secondly, and most importantly, who the target contacts are within the company. Decision making in companies (particularly on big-ticket, infrequently bought, or one-off purchase items) is often complex with multi-decision makers and influencers. The sales personnel should identify all the parties involved and pigeonhole them according to their roles. For example: gatherers of information, those designated to table recommendations on which decisions will be made, decision influencers, those party to the final decision, and the "buck stops here" final decision maker. The sales plan should cover all base points judged to be relevant in ensuring the decision goes your way.

The real challenge for the sales team is the complexity of customer decision making they are often confronted with and which they have to strive to manage. There is no such thing as a "single customer." Decision making is often an amalgam of individuals all pitching in but with their own personal slant on things. While they may individually be united by a common purpose, they can have contradictory and sometimes self-interested ways of achieving it.

It is superficial to refer to the customer as "the business" and the process being one of a "buying chain" because that suggests a tidy, sequential process. The reality is more of a messy combination of recommendations, consultations, committees, proposals, presentations, answering the same queries in triplicate, and multiple feedback loops where, seemingly, no single person can make a call but pretty much anyone can have a veto.

The other real challenge is how you handle the customer relationship. Selling emotional benefits is not the route to success, unlike that often being the preferred bridge to convert consumers in the B2C model. Yes, the customers in B2B have two personas: the human one and the professional one. But your efforts will be rejected, if not permanently damage your chances of ever crossing the drawbridge, if you focus on the emotional approach. The professional role will override the other and veto anything that doesn't clearly address them in a way that is clearly consistent with their job titles and their formal remit within the company they represent. So, the sales executive must find a way to rationally and professionally present a benefit led sales story that ticks all the boxes but manages to show a little empathy and connects with the audience on a personal level.

B. Lead management

The whole B2B CRM process starts with a lead—the name of the company you think you can sell something to. There's an entire process that flows from there before the lead becomes a customer. You need to identify a lead, qualify it, and only then convert the lead into a sale.

A lead can come from a variety of channels—website, cold calling, social selling, introduction via networking, word of mouth, recommendation, from attending an exhibition/seminar/conference, or purchased via a list.

Given the spread of sources, it is imperative that a policy is in place to determine which journey a lead will follow through the company according to the source it came from. It must be clear which person or department is ultimately responsible for logging in the lead because this channels how the lead should be routed and how it will be followed up on. Without a clearly defined work flow process, precious leads can easily end up lost or forgotten, which can result in management frustration, lost sales, and even a bad customer experience, or a combination of all three!

Once the lead is put into the system, the CRM software will then take it through the sales process. Each time you interact with the prospect, you record it into the system. The same applies if someone else ends up talking to the prospect.

It should be remembered that, apart from personal details, the CRM software also records what was discussed, what the next follow up is, status of an open action item, and so on. In a nutshell, CRM keeps track of all the lead related actions and what's been said and done.

At the same time, CRM acts as a library of documents plus calls and e-mails. A sales person directly enters any meeting or call notes onto the system. Equally, he or she can access the information logged against the prospect in preparing for a meeting or call. The system is there to support the sales person in making them more productive but also making their job more fulfilling. For example, the CRM system will remind the sales person to call at an agreed time. Sales teams working from home or traveling on business, can readily access and check data and instantly update it after a meeting.

When an interaction with a prospect is initiated, there is an instant, automated trail of communication. Moreover, because the information is in one central place, anyone in the company can engage in a dialogue with a prospect and help them in answering any queries.

CRM can help to automate a particular business process, as well as to automate the way each process works together with the other. But, as a statement of the obvious, each business process must be well defined and efficient to enable a company to achieve good results. It is the management team that directs the system, not the other way round!

C. Customer support

There needs to be clear rules for how customer service requests are managed. Such rules define, for example, whether a customer request goes to the first or second line of support, what resources will be used to solve a customer's problem and how status updates will be shared to ensure that the issue is being fully and properly addressed. Once the work flow and rules of engagement are defined and set, the CRM system can automate the whole flow.

At the same time, the system keeps record of the history of all the contacts, so that customer service teams can view the information to get a better understanding of how to help the customer, which can, in turn, be used to improve the customer experience.

D. Sales pipeline management

The system's functionality helps to manage the sales process from a commercial perspective. The status with a customer can be recorded and monitored from the initial prospect stage through to closing the deal. For example, prospects can initially be weighted according to their potential value and rating and/or seriousness of the enquiry. Thereafter, the status in the pipeline can be logged at each stage of the journey through proposals and/or quotes submitted, awaiting feedback/sign off, order confirmed, order placed, order invoiced, and so on. A coding system, such as a traffic light approach, can be applied at each stage to guide the degree of probability of progressing to the next stage. This can also include the ability to log the reasons for a final deal to be either won or lost and closed.

In this way, the company is far better placed to understand the sales pipeline, incoming prospects and, fundamentally, making forecasting simpler and more accurate.

E. Scoping the sales operation.

In evaluating which CRM solution to use, the company should scope out in detail its sales operation and processes, such as:

- What information is relevant at each stage of your sales process?
- Specification of the sales process: who does what and when, and their roles and responsibilities defined. This should embrace new business prospecting and managing and nurturing existing customers to maximize revenue potential and customer retention.
- How important is new business and repeat business to the company and what is the ranking of priorities?
- Key operational parameters. For example, number of times to make contact with a new business prospect before they purchase.

In overall terms, a CRM system gives you a clear overview of your customers. You can see everything in one place—a simple customizable dashboard telling you a customer's previous sales history with you, the status of their orders, any outstanding customer service issues and more.

Above all, however, it enables you to behave in a customer focused and friendly way.

What B2B customers want at an emotional level is to be treated as individuals. They want to feel like their business matters to you and that you care.

In B2B sales, a CRM system can make all the difference in whether or not you gain a new customer or retain an existing one. Customers who feel valued are more likely to be happy customers and happy customers mean repeat business.

Some Key Thoughts to Reflect on if You Are Considering/Reviewing CRM

A CRM business model and related systems and processes are a "shoo-in" for a B2B focused company.

All the principles and practices of CRM apply to B2B but "in spades." The sales and customer service functions come to the fore in B2B as the primary managers of the customer interface and the CRM system is designed to support them in every aspect of their roles.

In this context, CRM can add demonstrable value on two levels:

- It can enhance the chances of success in terms of converting a new customer and, thereafter, developing an ongoing relationship and related customer loyalty.
- It significantly improves the efficiency of the selling process with the twin benefits of minimizing the risk of "losing" a sale whilst improving productivity. The latter has the additional benefit of releasing sales managements' time from processing to focus on planning and "thinking."

Therefore, if you are working in a B2B model, you should consider the areas scoped out below to enable you to extract the maximum benefit from the CRM system. The important areas to concentrate on are the applications of the system and the human factors assuming you have designed, developed, and installed the CRM system to your specific requirements.

1. Is your sales team fully trained in "Persuasive Selling "—selling benefits and overcoming objections?

2. Have you coded all the customers (current and potential) into a business classification? In parallel, have you determined the universe size of the business classification and your penetration within it and, in turn, identified all the potential customers who you currently do not trade with?

3. Are all the customer details logged on the CRM system including profiles of all the contacts within the customer who can influence the buying decision? Their roles within the business and their personal "pen" portrait.

4. Do you have a formal process of lead management with related logging onto the system for all the details from the time the lead first enters the system to conversion (or non-conversion)? In so doing, do you positively use the CRM system to efficiently track leads and report on their status?

5. Do you use the CRM system to hold all the contact details with the customer including meeting notes, relevant telephone calls, correspondence, proposals, and so on—all held in a customer library?

6. Are all the transaction details held on the CRM system for each unique customer to give a single customer view?

7. Do you engage a formal sales pipeline management process with real-time, accurate reporting of the financial status of all the leads from the prospecting stage to closing the deal? Do you link this to sales forecasting using a probability weighting methodology to aggregate all the values to result in an overall forecast for company management to confidently use as their future sales barometer?

8. Do you have proper metrics in place to measure performance against the remit of enhancing customer experience? For example, a call should be answered within "X" minutes, a lead should be followed up within "Y" days. Are they incorporated in the CRM system?

CHAPTER 9

What Is Needed to Successfully Develop and Implement a CRM Strategy?

Earlier chapters have covered the various aspects of CRM development and implementation. Here is a summary of the key principles and practical steps that should be embodied in your approach to CRM. The foundations underpinning CRM, which, if not put in place, will mean you have not built a solid and robust CRM business model and related practices and processes.

Remember, above all, that developing and operating a CRM model is more than installing a software package. Fundamentally, it is a "top down" approach to business management. It involves all the functional areas of your business who need to be fully engaged and integrated into the CRM strategy and operating plan—human resources, marketing, sales, IT, product development, customer service, and so on.

The cornerstones of a successful CRM business model are given below.

Principles

1. At all stages, be objective, realistic, and honest in your approach. In particular, in your appraisal of where your business is in meeting customer needs and wants, your ability to adapt to meet them through product/service refinements/improvements, the operating support systems required to deliver them, the totality of the organizational structure to construct around a customer centric focus, and the critical path—action and timing—to achieve them.

2. Ensure you do not fudge decisions or fail to confront real issues and break down barriers impeding progress.

3. The Board of Directors should operate as a collective in buying into the CRM business model. In so doing, it must show vision, leadership, and positive enthusiasm and energy in communicating the CRM as a clear path to success for the whole of the company. They must all sing off the same hymn sheet in their messaging to all internal and external stakeholders. In many ways, adopting an evangelist posture in motivating staff members to sign up and follow the CRM banner.

4. Ensure all the company members understand CRM and what it means in your business.

5. To be transparent and regular in communication. CRM touches all the members of the company and they should all be party to the decisions made and the rationale behind them.

6. Formally review and evaluate progress at every step and adjust the tiller where necessary and/or remove any constraints or bottlenecks to pushing forward.

7. Base decision making on hard data. Make your decision judgements on quantified evidence and not "subjective feelings"; albeit the latter may be based on a number of years' experience working in the business.

Practical Steps

1. Build a comprehensive customer centric CRM model incorporating full customer segmentation embracing:
   - Defining the target customer audience—current and projected.
   - Segregate the target customer audience into segments based on their category and individual company/brand purchasing behavior.
   - Establish your current status by segment and in total, identifying strengths, weaknesses, opportunities, and threats.
   - Identify and quantify any differences in profiles, general attitudes, those attitudes and perceptions specific to the product/service category, and motivations across the segments.

- Define customer needs and wants and how, if at all, they vary by segment.
- Quantify the degree to which your current product/service meets their needs and wants relative to competition. In so doing, identify the features and benefits of the competing companies/brands within the category and any differential benefits currently enjoyed by any of them and also to enable you to identify any gaps.
- Build a customer segmentation model based on recency, frequency, and value to quantify the current sources of revenue and profit.

2. Conduct a comprehensive audit of all the customer data related processes and practices from data capturing through data storing to data reporting. In building a work flow model, identify where and how data is held, the frequency at which data is transferred between databases, which users are involved with any aspect of data, their roles, and how data is applied in the business.

   A key output is a map of the IT network for currently managing customer data, which also details any external suppliers and contracts involved in the support and maintenance of any component part of the network.

   In parallel, audit the current customer communications program laying down all the steps of campaign management from planning through execution to evaluation.

3. Identify all the elements of the current organizational structure involved in the customer management process: who, their roles and responsibilities, how they inter-relate, and so on.

4. Quantify CRM's future commercial objectives and other key performance indicators over a defined time horizon.

   This is absolutely crucial. The smooth implementation of CRM into the business is highly dependent on the level of planning that goes into developing a comprehensive strategy in the first place, which is obviously driven by the objectives. The clearer the CRM objectives are, the easier it will be to prepare a plan to implement the initiatives required to ensure all the employees understand how it relates to the overall success of the business.

5. Develop a written CRM strategy to meet the objectives covering:
   - The organizational structure
   - CRM software technical solution with written processes and procedures consistent with delivering "best practice" data security that is fully compliant with Data Protection Regulations
   - Product/service strategy to deliver any defined improvements required
   - Communication strategy to recruit, convert, retain, and develop customers to their optimum potential consistent with the objectives set
   - Reporting structure with timely and comprehensive reporting and evaluation of all the aspects of the CRM strategy; performance versus commercial objectives and other KPIs, campaign evaluations, monitoring changes in customer needs and wants, customer dynamics, and so on.
   - Data capture protocols; what data to capture, how and where to capture it
   - Identify all the capital costs involved with sourcing alternatives and the preferred option with payback
   - Identify all the operational costs including incremental new costs and cost savings and their time scale
   - Lay down communication plan to impart the CRM strategy to all the internal and external parties to embrace both initial and ongoing reviews and updates
   - Translate into a critical path with all the action points designated by time line
6. Company Board of Directors to formally sign off the CRM strategy.
7. Implement a comprehensive program to fully and properly communicate the CRM strategy and plan to all the internal company members and external stakeholders with follow-up feedback sessions in smaller groups.
8. Hold formal quarterly Board Reviews on progress isolating any corrective actions required and an action plan for their implementation. This should incorporate all the external customer data measurements and monitoring.

9. Hold regular departmental and/or company wide review sessions to communicate performance, progress, and issues arising.

Some Key Thoughts to Reflect on if You Are Considering/Reviewing CRM

Previous chapters have covered and interrogated the component parts of CRM. This chapter threads together the key principles and practices of CRM as your final summary check list.

If you can tick all the boxes listed under the "principles" of CRM and the "Practical Steps" you should follow in developing and implementing a CRM business model and related strategy, you should be well underway to give yourself the best chance of commercial success.

CHAPTER 10

CRM Benefits

The various business benefits associated with implementing different elements of the CRM approach to corporate management have been highlighted in the earlier chapters.

The benefits stemming from employing a CRM business model and strategy can be broadly divided into two camps: delivering the CRM central commercial goal of profit optimization and the various strands of benefits flowing from the working practices associated with it.

We summarize below the main benefits pertaining to both with, obviously, an overlap between the two given that they are complementary to one another.

Commercial Goal

Adopting the CRM business model is a primary route to the optimization of ongoing long-term company profits by:

1. Building a profile of the category "best customers" identifying those who demonstrate the greatest propensity to spend in the category.
2. Developing products/services that meet customer needs and wants, which are ideally superior to competition, enabling you to market a customer proposition that is benefit led.
3. Reaching and recruiting new "best customers" in the most cost efficient and effective way by using the profile developed as the target audience "pen" profile.
4. Increasing "share of wallet" among current best customers by maximising your share of your "best customers'" category spend, thereby building customer loyalty.
5. Nurturing a close relationship with "best customers" by fully using the customer knowledge available to you in communicating relevant

messages at the right time and at the right frequency. In so doing, using content and tone that connects with and engages customers in building a more personal "bridge" between you and your customers.

6. Increasing revenue and profitability from upselling and cross-selling where the opportunity to do so presents itself. Incremental revenue can be generated by providing additional products and services by productively using the customer knowledge acquired and held, and as customer satisfaction increases stemming from their improved and enriched customer experiences.

7. Customer attrition declines as customer loyalty increases. Receiving a higher level of more personal and relevant customer experience cements a stronger bond between you and the customer.

8. Cost savings are generated through improved productivity and employing targeted marketing techniques yielding "more bangs for your bucks." For example:

   - Sales teams are better placed to schedule and manage their time.
   - Sales and customer service teams are better able to respond to and solve customer queries.
   - There is a single, central customer database that everyone can access replacing the previous regime in which there were a multitude of spreadsheets held across departments; all holding essentially the same information but with slightly different definitions and formats.
   - The Customer Segmentation model enables marketing resources to be highly targeted against ROI criteria. Funds are focused on "best customers" with returns against low yielding customer segments (e.g., promiscuous buyers, low spenders) measured and support adjusted accordingly. This moves spend away from a "blanket approach" using "All customers are equal but some are more equal than others" as an overriding guide.

9. Supply of all relevant data is designed with one objective in mind: to enhance decision making. Some of the key features built into the data reporting and evaluation suite are:

   - Reporting in a timely manner with a focus on real-time reporting for key metrics.

- Reporting on all the KPIs that collectively represent the core variables in managing the business strategically and on a day-to-day basis. This will include measurements on sales pipeline status, sales forecasting, and revenue management by customer segment.
- External data measuring customer needs and wants.
- Monitoring company share status within the market category by segment versus objectives.
- Measuring customer dynamics by segment versus targets.
- Evaluating all the communication campaigns with ROI reporting.

10. Adopting a CRM Business Model, with a robust Operational Strategy in place, enables a company to maximize the upside and minimize the downside.

In the context of the latter, external events, outside a company's direct control, can directly impact a company's business in a profoundly negative and potentially catastrophic way.

Such events rarely occur but, when they do, they can kick in rapidly giving companies little warning and certainly no time to properly plan and organize themselves to deal with the consequences. The 2020 pandemic (Covid-19) is an example of this.

In such circumstances, companies can find themselves in reaction mode; making decisions in response to external factors that change on an almost daily basis.

In an ideal world, companies would have a contingency plan tucked away in their top right hand draw where they have simulated situations such as those. In reality, the vast majority, if not all, will not have done so. Having a CRM operational framework in situ will not cancel out the impact of such an event but it will dilute it because the company will have an element of control.

Such a customer centric company has its customers resident on their central database with their profile details and history attached to all. More importantly, they can engage in a two-way dialogue with them to get their feedback on how the event is affecting their current purchasing behavior and their future purchasing plans within the company's trading category. This, in turn, enables the company to tactically refocus and explore alternative routes to protect or, perhaps, expand short-term revenue streams.

In the UK, many companies switched resources to focus on internet buying where the opportunity to do so was present, with those already practicing CRM having a competitive advantage. One company that did not have to do so was Amazon; the arch-disciple of CRM, who was already in prime position to take advantage of the prevailing consumer mood to shop from home to avoid the risk of catching the virus!

Working Practices Benefits

- **Better customer relationships.** The more you know about them (and, importantly, are seen to know by them), the more you can structure relevant benefits to meet their needs and wants and, in turn, the more customers know you care about them. This enables you to forge a much stronger and deeper trading relationship.

- **Know your customers, close more sales.** Using the sales automation tools to track and monitor every customer's sales journey from start to finish in one place, enables the sales team to sell more efficiently and focus on delivering a good customer experience to help close the deal.

- **Improved ability to upsell and cross-sell.** The more you know about your customers' needs and wants, the better placed you are to put proactive ideas and solutions on the table; potentially leading to incremental sales.

- **Increased team collaboration.** This is conditional on company members buying into the CRM systems, being trained on and actively being measured on their system use. Everyone having access to the same data with a universal definition of all data will remove wasted effort and promote team integration and bonding. The customer becomes the only common focus removing departmental friction and information silos.

- **Improved customer interface.** Again, the more you know about clients, the better able you are to serve them. If everyone uses the CRM system properly in recording **every** customer interaction they have, then others are better able to service the customer utilizing the most up-to-date knowledge of everything discussed with the customer. This will impress, reassure, and primarily build customer confidence in dealing with you.

- **Greater staff morale and satisfaction.** The more relevant and helpful knowledge supplied to company members in an easily digestible and accessible way, the more empowered and engaged they are. Having an accurate and up-to-date CRM system that everyone uses and has access to helps company members solve customer problems and to sell-on. Doing so makes them and, in turn, the customers happy.

- **Less admin time, more sales time.** Providing data to give a single customer view means the sales team can focus on constructing the sales proposal to clinch the deal and not the record keeping. This is underscored with secure access and sharing of information.

- **Knowledge is power.** All the key team members have access to up-to-date data in real time. So everyone knows what's happening at any point in time. There is total transparency of the status in the sales pipeline with companywide visibility at company, team, and individual levels. Also, the role of forecasting is accentuated. Forecasting is more accurate with performance against forecast on all key metrics reported in real time. This yields an action orientated status report to enable critical decisions to hit targets but, more importantly, it spots where such action should be focused.

Some Key Thoughts to Reflect on if You Are Considering/Reviewing CRM

The pot of gold at the end of the CRM rainbow is the really significant commercial and working practice benefits stemming from the CRM business model.

This chapter summarizes the key benefits on offer as the prize for practicing CRM. The reader should use this as their reference to assess the degree to which they are realizing them within their own company and, if not, what they need to do to massage their own CRM business model.

It should also be noted that CRM is not one-way traffic. It can help companies minimize the downside as well as maximize the upside. Judgmentally, those companies with a CRM business model in place will have fared better in the 2020 Covid-19 pandemic than their competitive set. I encourage you to build this into your thinking and planning when considering or reviewing your CRM plans.

CHAPTER 11

Useful Measurement Definitions

Return On Investment (ROI)

Return on Investment (ROI) is a financial metric of profitability that is widely used to measure the return or gain from an investment. It is a simple ratio of the gain from an investment relative to its cost. It is used to evaluate the efficiency and effectiveness of an investment.

In CRM, it can be used to measure the effectiveness of an individual marketing or sales campaign or the payback on customer development.

Individual Campaign

This applies to any individual campaign, deployed against either acquisition or retention objectives, where there is a call to action connected to a measurable response on transaction value.

$$\text{ROI} = \frac{\text{Gross contribution}}{\text{Campaign cost}} \times 100$$

$$= \frac{\text{Net revenue} - \text{Variable cost}}{\text{Campaign cost}} \times 100$$

Notes

A. Net revenue = Gross revenue less VAT less any trading discounts
B. Variable cost = Costs of the product (e.g., raw materials, packaging, production cost, and distribution for a manufactured product) or providing the service
C. Gross contribution is a measure of gross profit equating to profit before sales and marketing cost, overheads, and contribution to net profit.

D. Campaign cost = Media cost (e.g., direct mail = creative design, creative production, materials, production of mailing piece, delivery) plus any incentive; for example, money off coupon. For the latter, ensure the cost is not double counted—it is either accounted for in the net revenue figure or in the campaign cost.

E. Any figure above 100 percent indicates a positive return.

Customer Development

In this scenario, we are looking at the payback period and associated return from the time a new customer is recruited. This incorporates the acquisition and retention costs where the latter is involved in nurturing an ongoing relationship; for example, loyalty program.

This is best illustrated by reference to a theoretical model based on a bottle of malt whisky. The relevant parameters are:

- Acquisition cost   = £7 per new recruit
- Retention cost   = £5 per customer per year covering the cost of the relationship marketing program
- Gross contribution   = £10 per bottle

The payback model per new recruit is illustrated in Table 11.1.

Table 11.1 Payback model for a new recruit

	YEAR 1	YEAR 2	YEAR 3
Acquisition cost	£7	£0	£0
Retention cost	£5	£5	£5
TOTAL COST	£12	£5	£5
Bottles bought per year*	0.75	1.5	1.5
Gross contribution	£7.50	£15	£15
Net contribution per year	(£4.50)	£10	£10
Cumulative net contribution	(£4.50)	£5.50	£15.50

*Incremental number of bottles bought per year

Notes

A. Break-even is passed in year 2 from when a positive contribution to profit is made
B. This simplistic model assumes a 100 percent retention rate. It will need to be adjusted to take account of the actual retention rate.

Customer Lifetime Value (CLV)*

Customer Lifetime Value is the total worth of an individual customer over the lifespan of their relationship with the company/brand—how much revenue to be made from an individual customer. It equates to the revenue an average customer will provide a brand/company before they discontinue their patronage. In this context, the simple formula to apply is to multiply the average annual revenue by the average lifespan of a customer as shown below:

Average annual revenue per customer x average lifetime of customer = Customer Lifetime Value

In reality, there are three factors that have an impact on the value:

- The purchase frequency of the product or service. For example, someone will buy food on a weekly cycle whereas someone may only decorate their house every 10 years.
- The lifespan of the purchase cycle. For example, someone may eat out at a restaurant at least once a year from the age of 22 years to the age of 75 years, whereas they only bought a baby buggy once in their lifetime at the age of 35 years. In this context, the annual purchase rate may vary at different life stages of the customer, which needs to be taken into account. For example, a customer's weekly supermarket shop will be potentially higher between the ages of 32 years and 55 years when children are at home than post children.
- The share of wallet a brand/company has of the customers' annual spend on the product/service category. This is a measure of brand loyalty with, obviously, 100 percent loyalty equating to the brand/company enjoying the full patronage of the customers' spend.

As a first step, it is important to evaluate the full potential worth of a customer across the possible lifespan of the customer being active in the product/service category—their total gross worth based on their total spend. This provides the ceiling of revenue opportunity based on 100 percent of the customer's spending on the category being with the individual brand/company.

This is illustrated below in Table 11.2 using a theoretical model based on the restaurant sector.

Table 11.2 Customer Lifetime Value calculation based on the restaurant sector

	AGE BREAKS: YEARS OLD						
	17–34	35–44	45–54	55–64	65–74	75+	TOTAL
Average annual customer value (£)	400	450	500	575	450	400	465
Number of years as a customer	13	10	10	10	10	5	58
Customer value by age break/cum (£)	5,200	4,500	5,000	5,750	4,500	2,000	26,950

Assumptions:

1. Customer first becomes a customer at the age of 17 years and will be an active customer until the age of 80 years.
2. Annual customer value reflects the average spend levels at the various life stages.
3. Values based on constant 2019 values with no allowance for inflation.
4. Note, the analysis is based on the average customer. As with any sector, there will be a heavy user segment where the potential returns will be correspondingly greater.

This analysis yields the potential lifetime value of a customer and should act as the reference point for strategic planning. For example, if your current share of wallet is 35 percent, an increase to 50 percent would yield an incremental lifetime value increase of £4,042.50 per customer. This would translate into an incremental revenue stream of £404,250,000 per 100,000 customers!

This demonstrates the strategic importance of using customer lifetime value as a KPI. Increasing customer lifetime value demonstrably increases the total value of the business and therefore the worth of the business.

It also ensures the strategic focus on three important customer dynamics:

1. Improving prospect to customer conversion
2. Reducing customer churn
3. Increasing brand share of customers' category spend (Share of wallet)

*(Bahman, Hajipour, and Molud Esfahani, Delta Model application for developing customer lifetime value, Emerald Insight – Marketing Intelligence and Planning, accessed October 8, 2018), (Baran, Zerres, and Zerres, Customer Relationship Management, Bookboon.co, accessed May 30, 2019), (Pfeifer and Bang 2005)

Customer Churn

This is one of the most important metrics in customer management and development; particularly for a company that is growing. It provides the quantified hard number on the harsh truth about your customer retention status. This was one of the failures of the dot.com boom in the late 1990s. Companies spent a shed load of money on customer acquisition (which made many an agency happy bunnies) but did not measure customer churn. They were managing a "leaky bucket" with customers, at great expense, entering at the top end but falling out at the bottom end.

The customer churn rate is the percentage of customers that stop using a company's product or service during a defined time frame.

It can simply be calculated by dividing the number of customers lost during the defined time period by the customer universe that was in place at the beginning of the time period.

For example:

Customer count at the beginning of the time period	= 5,000
Customer count at the end of the time period	= 5,250
New customers acquired in the time period	= 500
Customers lost in the time period	= 250
Churn rate	= 5%*

*5000–4750 = 250/5000 × 100 = 5%

Alternatively, revenue churn can be calculated over a defined time (say one year) period by:

- Annual running rate of value of business at the beginning of the year
- Annual running rate of value of business at the end of the year
- Number of new customers and revenue contribution

- Number of customers lost
- Value of recurring business lost
- Percentage of recurring value lost

Revenue churn reveals how much recurring revenue was lost in a given period of time. This is particularly important for a subscription business.

The churn rate and its management underpins a company's profitability on the proven premise that it costs more to acquire new customers than it does to retain the existing customers. There are many ratios quoted but, as a rule of thumb, a 5 percent increase in retention rate can increase profit by 25 percent because returning customers have a greater propensity to spend more on a company's products and services. This, in turn, gives the option for a company to spend less on acquiring new customers and saving related marketing cost.

Some observations:

- Identify those in your customer base who are most likely to lapse and why.
- Put in place a lapsing program targeting customers who are about to lapse. Once customers lapse, it is very costly to re-engage them if nigh on impossible.
- Be proactive in connecting with the segment who show lapsing characteristics. Communicate with them on all the benefits (emotional and functional) you offer and show them you care about their experience.
- Seriously evaluate the commercial benefits of pooling your resources into your loyal, profitable customers rather than prioritizing on offering more and more incentives to the customers who are considering churning.

Customer Acquisition Cost (CAC)

Customer acquisition cost is the amount of money spent on an individual recruitment campaign or across sales and marketing to close a transaction deal to recruit a new customer over a defined time period; for example, a company's trading year.

It is calculated by summing all the individual campaign costs, including any incentives offered, and dividing it by the number of new customers. Alternatively, summing a company's total sales and marketing spend against new customer acquisition and dividing it by the number of new customers recruited.

Amount spent on sales and marketing on new customer
recruitment in 2019 fiscal   = £X
Number of new customers acquired in 2019 fiscal   = Y
New customer acquisition cost   = £Z

Net Promoter Score (NPS)

NPS is a metric that can be used in measuring customer responses to any attribute where a quantified scale is used by grouping responses into three categories. Based on, for example, a 10 point scale:

Promoters   = those scoring 9 or 10
Passive   = those scoring 7 or 8
Detractors   = those scoring 0 to 6

The NPS score is derived by subtracting the percentage of "Detractors" from the percentage of "Promoters." This is simply illustrated below:

SCORING SEGMENT	COUNT	%
PROMOTER (9 or 10)	A	B
PASSIVE (7 or 8)	C	D
DETRACTOR (0–6)	E	F
TOTAL RESPONSES	G	100

NPS SCORE = % PROMOTER – % DETRACTOR

Anything above zero is good while anything below zero suggests action is required to address the issue being investigated.

The raw data is normally obtained by sending out a survey to the existing customers asking them, for example, how likely they would be to recommend your product or service to a friend, relative, or colleague?

In this context, a negative score will suggest you need to improve the customer experience with the survey indicating the areas you need to focus on for such improvements.

This methodology can also be used to gauge a "CUSTOMER SATISFACTION SCORE (CSA)" where the question in the survey is crafted to specifically address this.

Formula to Predict Response Rate Required to Break Even

Marketing costs are high and, as such, a scientific approach should be employed to build a response model to determine the response required to breakeven for a marketing activity in which a measurable transaction value is the object of the activity. The actual result can then be evaluated against the target required.

A very simplified model is outlined below based on a theoretical online consumer product as an example to illustrate the type of approach.

Formula

The breakeven point is where the communication cost equates to the gross contribution.

That is, cost of communications (comms) = gross contribution = net revenue × % profit margin.

Or net revenue = cost of comms/% profit margin

Net revenue = average order value (AOV) × number of orders (responses)

Therefore, for a predicted AOV, it is possible to derive the response required to breakeven.

Response rate required = Net revenue/AOV

For example, a model based on the following parameters:

- Contact universe   = 1,000

- Communication cost   = £2 per contact

- AOV   = £50

- % profit margin   = 45%

The formula works as follows:

1. Cost of comms (1,000 × £2 per contact) = £2,000
2. Net revenue = Cost of comms/% profit margin = £2,000/0.45 = £4,444
3. Net revenue = AOV × number of orders
   Number of orders = Net revenue/AOV

   = £4,444/£50 = 88.9 = 8.9% based on contact universe of 1,000

   Response rate required = 8.9%

Application of Formula

Table 11.3 shows how the formula is applied to the 3 levels of AOV and 3 levels of communication cost per contact; all based on a contact universe of 1,000:

Table 11.3 Application of formula to show response rate required to breakeven

COMMUNICATION COST		BREAK-EVEN REVENUE	AOV: RESPONSE RATE REQUIRED		
Per Contact	Total		£25	£50	£75
£1.00	£1,000	£2,222	8.9%	4.4%	3%
£2.00	£2,000	£4,444	17.8%	8.9%	5.9%
£3.00	£3,000	£6,666	26.7%	13.3%	8.9%

Some Key Thoughts to Reflect on if You Are Considering/Reviewing CRM

One of the major strengths of CRM is its focus on the commercial performance using quantified analysis to measure key metrics. This chapter features some formulae commonly used within the CRM fraternity; many of which are founded in Direct Marketing.

Readers should consider and incorporate them into their own analysis toolkit.

References

1.
Dr.G. Chuna Babu 2016
Cambra – Fierro, Centeno, Olavarria, and Vazquez – Carrasco 2017
Croteau and LI 2003
Greenleaf and Winer 2002
Kumar and Ramini 2004
Lun, Jinlin and Yingying 2008
Nweke (n.d.)
Payne and Frow 2005
Parvatiyar and Sheth 2002
Rababah, Mohd, and Irahim 2010
Rai 2014
Ryals and Knox 2001
Santos and Castelo 2010

2.
Dr. G. China, Babu 2016
Baharun 2008
Berry 1983
Collinger 2003
Evans and Laskin 1994
Malhan and Dr. Anjum 2017
Naderian and Baharun 2013
Ryals and Payne 2001
Santos, Almeida, and Monteiro 2003
Zikmund, McLeod, and Gilbert 2003

3.
Anderson, Fornell, and Mazvancheryl 2004
Dr. Angamuthu 2015
Arnold, Price, and Zinkhan 2003
Baharun 2008
Ballester and Aleman 2001/2005
Bowen and Chen 2001
Carev 2008

Malihan and Anjum 2017
Malthouse and Mulhern 2007
Naderian and Baharun 2013
Rather 2016
Salim 2018

About the Author

A Fellow of the Institute of Consulting, Mike Pearce's career spans senior positions in corporate management with "blue-chip" companies, management consultancies (including MD of an American Consultancy) and running his own businesses; all under the general umbrella of sales, marketing and CRM.

His career includes Executive and Non-Executive Directorships and working in and providing consultancy services to a wide spectrum of businesses—from large to small with a mixture of private and listed companies as well as setting up, developing and selling two companies.

The breadth and depth of his career experience has enabled him to witness the practical dimensions of CRM thereby placing him in a good position to draw insights on how to set up and execute a CRM strategy and its role in the business model.

Index

Letters '*f*' and '*t*' after page numbers indicate figure and table, respectively.

OTHER TITLES IN THE MARKETING COLLECTION

Naresh Malhotra, Georgia Tech, Editor

- *Stand Out!* by Brian McGurk
- *The Coming Age of Robots* by George Pettinico and George R. Milne
- *Market Entropy* by Rajagopal
- *Artist Development Essentials* by Hristo Penchev
- *Decoding Customer Value at the Bottom of the Pyramid* by Ritu Srivastava
- *Qualitative Marketing Research* by Rajagopal
- *Social Media Marketing* by Alan Charlesworth
- *Employee Ambassadorship* by Michael W. Lowenstein
- *Critical Thinking for Marketers, Volume II* by David Dwight, David Soorholtz and Terry Grapentine
- *Critical Thinking for Marketers, Volume I* by David Dwight, David Soorholtz and Terry Grapentine
- *Service Excellence* by Ruth N. Bolton
- *Relationship Marketing Re-Imagined* by Naresh Malhotra, Can Uslay and Ahmet Bayraktar
- *Marketing Plan Templates for Enhancing Profits* by Elizabeth Rush Kruger
- *Launching New Products* by John C. Westman and Paul Sowyrda
- *Smart Marketing* by Ahmed Al Akber

Concise and Applied Business Books

The Collection listed above is one of 30 business subject collections that Business Expert Press has grown to make BEP a premiere publisher of print and digital books. Our concise and applied books are for...

- Professionals and Practitioners
- Faculty who adopt our books for courses
- Librarians who know that BEP's Digital Libraries are a unique way to offer students ebooks to download, not restricted with any digital rights management
- Executive Training Course Leaders
- Business Seminar Organizers

Business Expert Press books are for anyone who needs to dig deeper on business ideas, goals, and solutions to everyday problems. Whether one print book, one ebook, or buying a digital library of 110 ebooks, we remain the affordable and smart way to be business smart. For more information, please visit www.businessexpertpress.com, or contact sales@businessexpertpress.com.

www.ingramcontent.com/pod-product-compliance
Lightning Source LLC
Chambersburg PA
CBHW061216220326
41599CB00025B/4658